HOW TO START AND GROW AN UKULELE GROUP

By Joshua Waldman,

Founder of The Tigard Ukulele Group

http://tigardukes.com

CORYLUS PRESS

Copyright © 2017 Joshua Waldman

Cover Design by Lauren Leslie

ISBN: 978-1546902737

NO PART OF THIS BOOK MAY BE REPRODUCED OR TRANSMITTED IN ANY FORM OR ANY MANNER, ELECTRONIC OR MECHANICAL, INCLUDING PHOTOCOPYING, RECORDING OR BY ANY INFORMATION STORAGE AND RETRIEVAL SYSTEM, WITHOUT PERMISSION IN WRITING FROM THE AUTHOR.

Table of Contents

INTRODUCTION   5
- *What to Expect in This Book*   8
- *How to Read This Book*   9
- *Join Our Online Community*   9
- *First, Evaluate Your Commitment*   10
- *Why Start a Local Ukulele Group Anyway?*   11
- *Disclaimer*   16

DECIDE ON YOUR GROUP'S FORMAT   18
- *Jam Session Format*   19
- *Frequency*   29
- *Group Size*   33
- *Picking Your Songs*   37
- *Song Resources*   41
- *An Important Note on Copyright Law*   43

TOOLS TO MANAGE YOUR UKULELE GROUP   45
- *Onsong*   48
- *Mailchimp*   50
- *Dropbox*   54
- *Facebook Private Group*   56
- *Website*   58
- *SEO Basics*   63
- *Tools Summary*   68

ORGANIZING YOUR FIRST MEETING   69
- *Finding a Venue*   70
- *Setting the Tone*   72

Jam Agenda	*77*
Staying Together	*81*
How to Lead Others	*85*
GETTING THE WORD OUT	**91**
Social Media	*92*
Partnerships	*97*
Posters & Community	*99*
Meetup.com	*102*
KEEPING UP THE MOMENTUM	**105**
Habits & Checklists	*106*
Join a Community of Other Leaders	*108*
Concerts	*108*
Community	*111*
Celebrate Your Successes	*114*
Mentoring Co-leaders	*116*
COMMON MISTAKES	**122**
Not Changing Your Songs from Time to Time	*122*
Talking About Politics or Religion	*124*
A Note About Race	*125*
Resources	**127**
Where to Find Songs	*127*
Checklists and Workflows for Running an Ukulele Group	*128*
Directory of All Groups	*135*
Acknowledgements	**187**
About Joshua Waldman	**188**
Join Other Group Leaders	**189**

INTRODUCTION

Recently, an ukulele friend came over to our house to play music with me. He told me that a newly formed group in the next town over is probably shutting down. The founder of the group had decided that playing a musical instrument just wasn't for her she was going to try Blues Dance next.

I didn't know to laugh or to cry so I gaped at her instead.

"Really, People do that?"

Her group had 15 regular members and was the only one in that town. It made me really sad to hear about its imminent collapse. I pressed further to try and figure out what had gone wrong (besides retirement "hobby ADHD").

First, they met only monthly. Several of my new members came to my group from her group because we met weekly and they were looking to play more frequently. She didn't seem to understand the desires of her group's members.

Second, they didn't have anyone to lead them in song. They used a song circle format with a group of beginners who don't know each other. Song circles work well with smaller groups or groups of very experienced musicians. They seem to collapse when everyone is new. It puts a lot to pressure on people who only want to play and don't want to be responsible for the song.

Thirdly, not only was the website terrible (think about scrolling marque GIF banners from 1996 AOL websites), it was taking many hours of her time to organize each monthly meeting. There is a better way and I'd like to show you how.

When I started The Tigard Ukulele Group (TUG) in 2015, I made many mistakes. Over the years, I've learned a lot about what to do and what not to do when it comes to starting and continuing a successful ukulele club.

I love playing the ukulele. I love the joy it brings to people's lives. Hearing about the demise of this other club motivated me to put some of my ideas to paper and share them with anyone willing to read them.

The most important lesson, and one that I never anticipated learning, was about leadership.

For most of my life, I've never been the first one to raise his hand, never been the first one to volunteer, or ask a question during a meeting. Even as a Boy Scout, my adult leaders always told me I was the type to lead from behind. If someone else took my idea, I'd be content knowing that at least the idea had life.

TUG was only supposed to be an external motivator to keep me practicing the ukulele — a chance to play more songs more often with more people.

After two years of experimenting with frequency, format, tone, leading songs, marketing and organizing events, I've learned that the success of your group is *you*. You are the founder, or at the very least, their leader. Without your leadership and commitment, your group won't last. Notice I didn't say "ability to play the ukulele" because that has nothing at all to do with it.

If I had known I'd be leading songs, organizing a song book with hundreds of tunes and arranging concerts, I don't know if I'd have done it. But I have to say, I'm glad I did. Getting pushed out of your comfort zone isn't always something I seek, ask my wife who literally has to beg me to go on vacations. It is, however, the best way to learn about one's self and grow as an individual.

What you'll find in these pages are the painful truths and nuggets of wisdom I've learned on my journey to bandleader. You'll learn the options for finding a venue and communicating with the group, we'll roll up our sleeves and get very technical with the tools available, and I'll share some of the bloopers and mistakes to watch out for so you can have as much fun as possible starting and growing your ukulele group.

What to Expect in This Book

Having written a For Dummies book, I'm very good at breaking complex ideas into small, manageable parts. Like learning a new piece of music. At first it seems impossible, but when you focus on one measure at a time, after awhile, you have a whole song.

Well, the same is true with starting your new ukulele group. As a whole, the idea of running a group may be daunting, but when broken apart into small, manageable chunks, you can totally do it. Anybody willing to put in the time can.

What I'm going to present here is how I've done it. This is not the only way, certainly not "the right way". There is no "right" way to run an ukulele group. The "right" way is what works for you and for your members. My group meets weekly, plays and repeats 10 songs in two hours and I pick what we play each week. Other groups are completely the opposite, meet monthly, play 20 songs one time through in three hours or use a song circle format. That's fine. It's the diversity of this format that makes it fun for everyone.

When you're reading these pages, know that I'm not being prescriptive. However, I will get very technical at times showing step-by-step instructions for some technologies so that you can make your own informed decisions. At other times, I'll tell you stories of what worked and what didn't so you can make up your own mind.

How to Read This Book

You can read this book cover to cover. In fact, if you're brand new, just starting a group or only considering it, I'd suggest that kind of read. The order of the chapters, more or less, will be linear to your group's nascent formation.

On the other hand, because I've written this like a reference manual, you are welcome to pick the chapter you want to learn about and only read that. I'll do my best to not refer too much to earlier chapters. If you already have a group and are looking for ideas to grow it, then this will probably be how you read this book.

Join Our Online Community

As a reader of this book, I'd like to invite you to join our online community of other uke group leaders. Here we will share ideas, inspire each other and help keep up the momentum.

Join us by going here: http://www.tigardukes.com/leaders

First, Evaluate Your Commitment

Don't start this if you're not ready to put in at least a full year. They say most businesses fail within their first two years. So, asking you for a year is being generous! Especially since running an ukulele group is fun and rewarding - and you don't have to think about your bottom line.

Any new endeavor takes commitment. If you're not ready to put some effort into your group, you'll wind up disappointing a lot of people. That being said, if you give it a year and it doesn't work out, fine. But I've seen groups get started, develop lots of momentum, and then the leader gets bored. Well, there are 30 uke players now looking for a place to play together.

We'll talk about succession planning, so don't think you have to run your group forever. My definition of success is creating a group that lives beyond me that can still operate if I need to take a week or two off, or that will continue whenever I'm ready to have my Sunday afternoons free again.

My proudest moment as a group leader was handing the meeting off to someone I trusted, then hearing how wonderful it was when I got back. Way to go!

Maybe you're not able to give that kind of commitment, so perhaps it's a good time to share this book with a co-leader who has your vision of building a fun ukulele community and can share the responsibility. Sharing this project could be really fun! And you won't have to be the only one making this one-year commitment.

If it wasn't for my wife, Lily, and her support, I'm not sure I would have had the patience to grow our group from seven folks in our living room to 30+ people at the Grange hall each week.

So, who's got your back?

It's ok if you don't have a co-leader yet, or a support person. They will come. Keep your eyes open for the person not laughing at you!

Why Start a Local Ukulele Group Anyway?

Steven Sinek wrote a book called, "Start with Why." In it, he shares many leadership and success stories that all have that one thing in common; the leader started their project, business, software company, with the simple and powerful question, "Why?"

What is your *Why* for starting an ukulele group?

It's incredibly important to have this answered clearly before starting.

Here are some of the reasons I decided to start the Tigard Ukulele Group (TUG).

Play More

If you're like the rest of us ukulele enthusiasts, we simply want to play more! But let's face it; there are only so many hours you can sit in front of your favorite YouTube ukulele teacher before getting bored. There are only so many hours you can work on your scales, or your James Hill songs.

At some point, you just want to play music! You long for that flow, that feeling of knowing a song so well that you watch yourself while you're playing and singing it.

Sure, the more you play, the better you get. But on a more fundamental level, it's fun to play.

Playing more means having more fun with your ukulele. What's wrong with that? This is a great reason to start an ukulele group.

Learn to Play With Others

When you're sitting in your living room, song sheet in front of you, and you're jamming away, all is good. As a living-room soloist, you have total control over your music. If you want to slow it down, go for it. If you want to speed it up and build intensity, fine.

But the second you try to play with other people, that kind of playing will go sideways. There's a skill in being able to play with others, in listening, in keeping tempo, in accompanying soloists, in soloing and being accompanied. You might not have aspirations to be a professional musician, but at some point, either at a uke festival or when your guitarist friend comes over, you will need to be good at playing with others.

Build Community

One important aspect of the Tigard Ukulele Group was the community we built. This wasn't my *Why* at first, but community has become my *Why* over the years.

They say one of the biggest contributors to living a long and happy life is feeling a part of a community. I've always felt like an outsider. But for the first time, I feel like I belong somewhere.

Our uke club has inside jokes, shared history, holiday parties, fundraisers, and more. We've come to rely on each other for friendship and music each week. I'm constantly floored at the generosity and kindness of our members.

Last winter we had terrible snow. One of our longtime members Sande fell and broke her elbow on her way to the car. She couldn't join us for months. But at home, she played (or tried to!) the songs we had each week. Then, when she came back, everyone chipped in to get her flowers and a card.

If this is something you'd like to have in your life too, then know that you can build it.

Leadership

Leadership is an interesting thing. In an age that seems to value collaboration and groupthink as ultimate ideals, real leadership seems to be based on how rich you are or how charismatic you are. I think this is a sad waste. Everyone has leadership potential. Despite our media, human nature is human nature, and groups of humans seek out a leader to represent them. The world isn't run on consensus or on who has the most likes.

Being a leader requires you to find your self-confidence, own the room, make decisions and take risks. It also means potentially making public mistakes and embarrassing yourself. But it also means being someone that others can rely on, being the beacon that guides people, of taking the initiative on fun and inspiring projects.

When I started TUG, I had no interest in leadership. I work for myself in a home office. My business is online and I don't have a team to manage, nor do I have a boss to worry about. I'm not trying to be a better boss or climb some corporate ladder. What does leadership have to do with me?

What I learned is that leadership is a very personal journey. It's a mirror for your own limiting beliefs, low self-esteem, self-doubt and fears. One of the greatest benefits of having started this group has been the chance to face these parts of myself and deal with them and then grow as a person.

We were working on a difficult and highly orchestrated song one time when a longtime member who hadn't been for a while showed up. She hadn't been there the previous two weeks while we were working on this. When she raised her hand and had some suggestions that would have radically changed what we'd been doing for weeks, I shut her down. "It is the way it is. No more changes," I said and then watched as she shut down, stopped playing and her body folded in on itself.

I immediately realized my mistake, having gotten so intensely focused on getting the song right that I forgot that we were there to have fun! After the session, I went up to her and apologized. Although she shook it off, said it was no problem and changed the subject, I could tell she appreciated the apology.

Leadership isn't always easy. But it does make you a better human being as long as you learn from your mistakes.

Leadership might not be your *Why* at first, but I'm willing to bet that it will soon become very important to you.

Happiness

Everything we've talked about so far — playing more uke, building community, musical conversation, finding your inner leader — add up to you being happier.

Maybe your *Why* is: **Be Happier**

Why not?

This is not only a constitutionally mandated pursuit, it's perfectly achievable through the organization of your own ukulele club.

The Dalai Lama said that the more you are interested in the happiness of others, the happier you will be. Your group has the potential to not just make you happier, but will make others happy, which in turn will make you happy. It's a beautiful cycle of kindness and giving.

It all starts with you making the commitment to start your ukulele group.

Disclaimer

Please know that I'm writing this book from my own experience and am suggesting this as only one way to do things. Please make your own decisions about how to start and grow your ukulele group. I'm neither a doctor nor a lawyer, nor do I play one on TV.

As for grammar, you may have noticed I'm using "an ukulele" rather than the grammatically correct "a ukulele". Sorry about that. Well, not really sorry. The Hawaiian way to saying "ukulele" sounds like "oo-koo-le-le" which changes the sound of the word from how many mainlanders say it, "Yu-ka-ley-li". Since the OO sound has the "an" particle, I'm breaking English to make it happen that way on the page. Also note that "Uke" sounds like "Yuke" and therefore will get the "a" particle.

Also, in some areas in this book I talk about technologies and software products. Often, I give you my affiliate link with those mentions. What this means is that if you click the link from this book and eventually decide to sign up, I get some kind of benefit, whether it's more storage, extra features or some cash. In any case, I never recommend something to you I don't use myself. And supporting me in this way doesn't cost you anything. I thank you in advance for using my affiliate links.

DECIDE ON YOUR GROUP'S FORMAT

Although you don't have to have all the answers to how your group will look and how it will run up front, it does help to consider these things right away. After all, it's your group. It can be whatever you want. For me, it took a while to realize this and to take charge in making these decisions. In the following sections, I'll discuss group format, frequency and size in great detail. Will you have a song circle or sit in rows, will you meet weekly or monthly, will you be a small or large group? Eventually, your vision for your group will emerge. These are the three biggest considerations to keep in mind.

Jam Session Format

You may find that the format for your group changes over time. Over the years, I've added new elements to TUG that have worked well. Feel free to experiment with the formats described in this section.

When you start your group, pick a structure and give it a few sessions. Then take an honest assessment both with yourself and your members. Do you want to keep it? Try something totally different? Or just add new elements to it.

Quality vs. Quantity

The first few jam sessions with TUG had felt underwhelming. We went through the songs once, and many sounded like a train wreck. Granted most of the problem was that I was so new to playing the instrument. We already had a strong divide between the noobs like me and the extremely experienced players like John, a member who has been playing music for over 50 years.

Looking back, what seemed to have happened with the song circle format for us was that the experienced players would bring in songs at their level, which I found very difficult and could only play every third chord. And the new players, we would bring in our C-F-G songs, which would bore everyone else.

With a group of our small size and diverse skill level, especially at the beginning, the open format simply didn't work.

Then, as part of the agreement for using the Grange's space, we had to perform at their spring garden party. This meant our jam sessions started to look more like rehearsals. For our 30-minute set, we picked ten of our best sounding songs, songs that we felt the audience could sing along to. For two hours during the weeks preceding the concert we played and replayed those ten songs. We focused on being able to start cleanly and all together. We focused on being able to end all at the same time. And we focused on playing softly when our harmonica player took his solo. In short, we were looking for performance ready material.

After a while of this new format, I checked in with the group to see if they were getting tired of this. To my surprise, everyone really appreciated it. This format continued naturally, even after the concert. In fact, to this day, if a song could have gone better, and I'm about to flip to the next one, members will ask to repeat it, "just one more time."

After that concert, I noticed that week after week, we continued to get better at our songs, smiling more while playing and feeling more connected as a group. For instance, a little eye contact before a tricky ending that we'd been struggling with over the last few weeks communicated our shared experience, reassurance that we were determined to get it right this time and a mutual friendliness that we're all in this together.

Yes, we ended up not playing as many songs during our two-hour meetings. But we felt WAY better about the songs that we did play.

So when you're deciding on the format of your group, consider carefully what's important to you; going through as many songs as possible or repeating songs so that people feel more confident playing together.

This isn't as much of an issue with a more experienced group who can breeze through tough songs perfectly. Chances are members of a new ukulele group will have the kind of diversity we had.

I know that most ukulele groups don't repeat songs. And if that's been your experience and you like that, then just make that a conscious decision.

But know that there is another way. That if you like, you can work on beginnings and endings of songs, and re-do difficult passages. Know that your members will follow your lead. So, don't feel like you have to keep things moving in order to keep interest. It's been my experience that many uke players would rather gain confidence by mastering fewer songs, than feel flooded by too many.

If you have a group of very experienced players, go for as many songs as you can fit. Your members will be able to keep up. But if you have a group of inexperienced players or a wide range of experienced people, take your time and focus on learning the songs well. Don't be afraid to repeat a song once or twice to polish the beginnings, endings, difficult passages or challenging chord progressions.

The Kanikapila Song Circle

Kanikapila is Hawaiian for "song circle", though the term is used loosely in many uke clubs to just mean "jam session" or "meeting".

Traditionally, these are small gatherings of musicians and dancers at a community center or someone's house. Someone starts a song, others pick up on it, there's some eye contact, someone takes a solo, then there's some more eye-flashing, another solo, the song repeats and everyone had a great time!

To be able to do this you need to:

- Be an experienced musician
- Know, generally, the song being played
- Feel comfortable with your fellow players

These days, a "song circle" is literally that, a group of players sitting in a circle where someone brings a song and leads the group in playing it.

This format is easy to organize. The leader doesn't need to prepare anything. The work of leading songs is shared among everyone in the group. For new uke players, this format can't be any simpler.

Also, this is a great way to let people feel involved. They get to share with others the songs they love, and maybe get to show off a little bit.

There are some concerns to remember with this format however:

- If the members of the song circle are also newbies, the songs might not flow very well
- If the leader of the song is new to music, the rest of the group may not have clarity around what to do
- The circle is over as soon as you all run out of songs. That means smaller groups need to bring more songs.
- There's a size limit to how many people this will work for. We found that more than 15 people make a song circle more difficult
- You often won't have a chance to play the same songs from week to week, since most people will want to bring in new stuff

We started TUG out this way. But as we grew and as we had the pressure to perform, we dropped the song circle until the last 30 minutes of our session. That last half-hour, anyone can bring in anything, they can do a solo, bring copies of songs they want to lead or do a dance! (Yes, we've danced in our Kanikapila time.)

We like it when people bring new songs and we want them to feel like they are contributing, which they are. After all, some of those new songs people bring in are wonderful and I'll incorporate them into the more structured part of our meeting later on.

Orchestration

Sometimes uke clubs get a bad reputation for being "strum and hums". There you are, one of 50+ people, playing as hard as you can just to hear yourself. Everyone is singing the same notes. Everyone is strumming the same chord shapes in the same pattern. Sure, it can sound big, but it doesn't necessarily sound musical and your fingers hurt after a while!

The idea of orchestrating a group of musicians is as old as big-band, bebop, doo-wop, and heck, let's go back to the Baroque era while we're at it.

Think about a symphony. There are sections, a rhythm section, a string section, horns, woodwinds and so forth. These sections play smaller and different musical patterns such that, together, they create a larger musical experience for the audience. For example, the mandolin orchestra in Portland all play the same instrument. But, they are orchestrated, making them sound beautiful and full of emotion.

With a group of ukuleles, they seem to all have a similar musical quality, the same range of notes and the same timbre. However, there's a lot you can still orchestrate like picking patterns, strumming patterns, chord voicing, and of course, vocal harmonies.

I'm not a trained musician, music teacher, conductor or composer. However, I have tried to teach my ukulele group orchestrated songs. It's more work, sure, but it sounds great!

What I'm going to share with you are some ideas that a non-trained musician can do to create some cool sounding orchestrations. If you want the real deal, head on over to Ukustration:

https://tablelandukulelegroup.wordpress.com

Or take one of the Keins' workshops:

http://quietamericanmusic.com

Also, James Hill sells several orchestrated scores, most cost around $20:

http://www.ukuleleintheclassroom.com/catalog

There are several key areas that can be easily orchestrated:

- The lick as in the melodically definable riff of the song, such that when you hear it, you're like, "Oh! I know that song!" Think of Johnny Cash's *Ring of Fire*
- The chord voicings - there are many ways to play the same chord and when two ukes play the same chord differently, it can be sweet like corn chowder
- Vocal harmonies - we're not a Gregorian chanting choir droning on, in fact even the Gregorians have better harmony than what our group used to sing like. Ask your more vocally talented members to try singing the harmony (rework)
- Call and response- not everyone has to play or sing every line. Many songs have a natural split between callers and responders, left side versus right side, or boys vs. girls

I don't think it's practical to orchestrate every song you do, however, adding one each session could spice things up.

If you'd like to see TUG doing an orchestrated version of *Ring of Fire*, check out this video: https://youtu.be/hLHcKO3P3oA

Notice the picking pattern and the strumming. The more advanced members play the picking pattern while everyone else strums and sings. The results are a much more dynamic and pleasant sounding song. (If you listen to the whole video, you'll hear me giving directions, calling out the repeat of the chorus and the tag; another technique for leading songs you can use.)

Adding the lick to a song can really enliven it and adding patterns to songs isn't as hard as it looks.

If you can read music, it's easy enough to find the sheet music of the song you want to orchestrate. Find the lick, or riff, in that song, and put it into tablature so everyone in the group can read it and figure out where in the song it belongs. Many songs only have a lick at the beginning, the bridge and the end.

Don't over complicate this and certainly don't expect everyone in your group to be able to read notation. Make it simple.

If you don't read music, it isn't a problem. There are several options you have. First, is good old listening. Ear training, is being able to pick out a melody from listening to it, and is an extremely rewarding skill. It allows you to turn a piece of music you enjoy hearing to something you can play along with at home. Find a recording of the song you want to orchestrate and try to figure out what notes are being played in the lick. Here, the pause button is your friend. Listen to the notes in the song, pause, find the note on your uke, then move on to the next note.

Another thing you can do is look for a YouTube tutorial on that song. You can take the main, definable piece of the tutorial, turn it into tablature and teach it to your group.

I realize this is additional work, and probably something you've never tried to do before. So why not see it as an experiment. Who knows, maybe someone from the group will love the idea and take it over.

Linear

This format is about as simple as they come. A leader, not members, picks an arrangement of songs and leads them in front of rows of players, and you go through them one at a time until the end.

The Portland Ukulele Association follows this model, and has done so for over a decade as does the Austin Ukulele Society.

The San Jose Ukulele Club follows this model, however, instead of having a single leader for all the songs, members volunteer to stand up and lead a song each meeting. They see this as a performance and prepare to lead their song seriously. So a two-hour jam might have 20 songs, but 20 different people will have led it. I think this is only possible when your group has reached a certain size, however.

Virtual

This winter we had an uncanny amount of snow in the Portland area. Overnight, almost a foot of snow fell shutting the city down. Portland doesn't have very many snowplows. The ones they have are used only on main roads and highways. Businesses were closed and almost no one was out and about. By Friday, it was clear to me that I'd have to cancel our ukulele jam, which I really didn't want to do.

I'd seen several Facebook Live posts by then and did some research on how to set one up for our private group. Turns out broadcasting a live video feed via Facebook is really easy, all I needed was a mobile device with the Facebook app loaded on it.

When I sent my Mailchimp email with our songs, I notified the group that we were meeting virtually this Sunday, that, "the snow was not going to stop us from playing the ukulele!" The instructions were to come over to my house if you could (some members lived a walking distance away) or if not, tune into our Facebook Group at the regular time and be prepared to play along at home.

So I lit a fire in our fireplace, arranged our folding chairs in a semicircle around the iPad and mounted it on a stand facing the fire. At 2pm, I hit "Start Live Stream" and had Lily check her phone for comments.

It was a huge success. Over 30 people participated in the stream. In between songs they sent comments, which Lily read out loud. Everyone on the stream was playing along at home. And the recording stayed in our Facebook group for latecomers to catch up.

All of this is to say that running a virtual ukulele group is not only possible, but also very viable. Cynthia Lin, Aldrine Guerrero and other teachers run regular virtual jam sessions. If you live in a place where weather gets in your way, or where people have to drive long distances to get there, consider using Facebook or YouTube to broadcast your jam sessions live.

Frequency

One of the main reasons I wanted to start an ukulele group was to practice the instrument as often as possible. Having played in several bands during high school and college, I knew it would take weekly practice to become even a little competent, get to know my band mates and feel confident playing in public.

There were other groups in the area that met monthly. They were relatively far away and very large. Often over 80 people would attend. The few times I went, I felt drowned out and didn't really have fun. At the end, my fingers hurt because I'd unconsciously played my uke harder just to hear myself.

I made some quick decisions about my group, which turned out to be the right decisions for me. First, I wanted my group to be smaller, which I'll talk more about that in the next section. Second, I wanted to meet weekly, which I'll talk about in this section.

When you're deciding on the frequency of your group, please consider the options carefully.

First, what's your level of commitment? Using the tools I describe in a later section, it only takes me 30 minutes to plan for and organize our weekly TUG meetings. I knew I wouldn't need a lot of time to do this, however, I needed to check my commitment to a weekly frequency. At first, I didn't think I could do it. You may be thinking, "Weekly? Are you kidding?" The truth is, if you are serious about your uke, there's not a better way to do this.

Second, what are your goals? Do you want to get better? Do you just want to hang out and have a good time?

Third, how much time can you actually spend leading this? You may want to spend your weekends gardening, not schlepping gear to a venue and running a group of amateur musicians. You might travel a lot and don't want to tie up your weeknights.

Another big consideration is meeting time. Karen Snair, an amateur ukulele player and freelance writer in Montreal, Quebec, Canada reminded me to:

> *Make sure the meeting doesn't conflict with other ukulele clubs in the area. If it does, it could look bad so be careful when selecting*

a time to meet. In my area, there are several groups that meet on different nights. Three different ukulele clubs meet on three different evenings: Monday, Tuesday, and Wednesday evening in different parts of the city. This prevents members from having to choose between which club they wish to attend. What happens is that sometimes members will go to more than one club during the week, which is okay because every group is different and special.

In the following sections, I'll explore the pros and cons of a weekly versus a monthly meeting. But at the end of the day, how often your group meets comes down to what you're willing to do. Make the decision carefully at first, as it can be hard to change this once the group starts.

Weekly

Over the last two years of running TUG, our weekly format has won the loyalty of many of our members. Often, new arrivals will tell me, "I was looking for a group that met more often than the other ones [monthly]." I'm convinced our weekly format has helped us acquire dedicated and serious players, which has made leading the group way easier.

Each week we have a nice mix of dedicated members who never miss, drop-in members who come when they can, and new members who are only looking around. This is a nice combination because our regular members can carry the song and the new players don't feel so much pressure to "get things right".

Before you discount a weekly meeting, consider the following:

- Weekly groups often attract more serious players, which makes your job as leader that much easier
- They don't take much more time to organize than monthly groups. What's an extra 30 minutes of your time each week to choose songs and send an email?
- Weekly meetings will make *you* a better play *fast*
- Weekly meetings will make *you* a better leader *fast*
- If you want your group to play in public, weekly meetings will get you performance ready in short order

Monthly

The Portland Ukulele Association (PUA) meets monthly and they've been around for over 15 years. In contrast, another local monthly group is in a leadership crisis and will likely disband in less than a year. Anecdotally, there doesn't seem to be a correlation between a group's success or failure based on the frequency of their meetings. If you feel that monthly is just about all you can commit to, feel free. Keep the following in mind:

- It might actually take you more time organizing a monthly group than a weekly group because you won't have the repetition and habits that make organizing the event easy

- Your group will likely be larger than weekly groups. See the next section for a discussion on group size to see if that's really what you want
- You may get a lot of new members, which means your job as a leader is much more difficult and you may be carrying the song on your own much of the time
- You may not be able to tackle more challenging songs, since they often require more practice than simple three-chord tunes

With these things in mind, remember that how often your group meets is a function of your time availability and commitment, and at the end of the day, only you can decide those things.

Group Size

Have you seen videos on YouTube of some of the larger ukulele groups playing? One large group I like to listen to is the Austin Ukulele Society. I've counted 50+ people in their midst on some recordings. It looks like so much fun to be a part of! Everyone is smiling, playing together, and really seem to be enjoying themselves.

Conversely, smaller groups like the Ukulele Orchestra of Great Britain have a subtlety in their playing impossible to find in larger groups. Of course, wouldn't it be great to play as well as UOGB and make such beautiful, delicate music!

Group Size

When starting your group, think carefully about the size of the group you'd like to have.

I'm an introvert. I like to make connections with individuals. I like to play my instrument gently. These factors went into choosing to cap my group at 30. Luckily, I've never had to turn anyone away. We've never gone over that number. But if we did, I'd have to start asking for RSVPs. Something simple like, "Reply YES to this email if you plan to attend." This would allow me to do a headcount and limit attendance if I had to. I'm 100% willing to do this in order to preserve the purpose of TUG. When you pick your number, it needs to be something you can really stand by and justify to someone you're turning away for the betterment of the group.

The feedback from our regular players is supportive of that decision. I hear this a lot, "I love the size of this group, please don't let it grow much bigger."

This size allows us to sit in a circle, which feels more like a community to me, and less like a performance.

Also, quite selfishly, I wasn't a very experienced or confident player when I started TUG (it's very debatable that I am now!). I wasn't interested in sitting in front of 50+ people, all eyes on me, microphoned, and feeling pressure to play the song right like some kind of band leader. With a small circle, we are all equal. I'm free to mess up. Others are free to step up. Everyone can hear themselves and everyone else. Over 30 people and the circle doesn't work.

If fact, we had 29 people come once and funny thing happened. Because everyone was listening to the person next to them, there was a wave effect with the songs. I'd finish and then a moment later, the people across from me would finish. We looked at each other and shrugged. The next time we had such a large group, we used two semi-circles as our layout, which worked much better.

If you aren't an experienced player, I'd highly recommend this smaller circle format. However, if you are a competent musician and confident in your ability to lead people in songs; go for a larger group where you'll be miced and standing in front of rows of attendees. Many uke clubs use this format very successfully, for example, the San Jose Ukulele Club. Each week, members step up to the mic and lead a song with the group leader organizing who those people will be.

Of course, if you are a competent bandleader, you probably aren't reading this book :)

Chontel Klobas is the founder of the well-known ukulele group in Seattle called STRUM, which stands for Seattle's Totally Relaxed Ukulele Musicians. She's studied with Uncle Rod Higuchi who helped her start her group. They run four groups on Facebook which you can find by searching STRUM, and can be found online here: strumseattle.com. Her group grew very quickly and she had a very interesting way of handling it. Here's what she told me about managing group size:

> *STRUM has grown to be may things, and it is managed by identifying these group of interest with a sub name. We have over 60 plus*

members now, and I do not want to become paralyzed by volume, or ever turn anyone away that wants to play ukulele with us.

So I added different groups based on interest to help control growth, and to allow many players to shine in areas that they love. I let others lead them, but keep a pulse on them since they have the STRUM name.

For example:

STRUM Song circle is the main group that meets weekly; Winter inside, Summer outside!

STRUM "Friday Nights and I ain't got nobody" is jam at a local restaurant. It's for intimate discussions, working out new songs; some other musicians often join us, violin, mandolin, guitar players etc.

STRUM STRINGS is a monthly group that works on growing skills rather than jamming, its not for everyone, but this group has really made great progress

STRUM on the road again is the performing part of STRUM. I find most gigs work well with four up to twelve players. Any more and the sound dilutes. This group plays gigs often so the beginning and endings of songs are very tight and they have a blast!

STRUM Outreach is for ukulele players who enjoy playing at Children's Hospital, Hospice, and Veterans homes. Intimate playing. *Not for all, but wonderful group that enjoys this way of sharing ukulele.*

STRUM Berries *is a group that enjoys exploring baritone ukuleles.*

Picking Your Songs

When TUG first started, we went around the circle and everyone brought a few songs to lead. When we were seven people in my living room that was fine; but we soon grew out of that format and I had to start making decisions about what songs we'd play that day.

I experimented with a few ideas. First, I tried having the same opening song and closing song each session. After a year, folks were getting tired of those tunes. So I ditched that.

Next, I played around with song order and noticed that if we played the more difficult songs first, the new players got discouraged and gave up sooner.

I arrived at the following conclusion: when picking songs for the jam, the first three to five songs should be the easiest, then they can get progressively harder. New or difficult songs should go last.

Ergo: start with easy songs then get progressively harder and introduce new songs last.

Picking Your Songs

By "easy songs" I'm talking about two to three chord songs, often with the C-F-G progression. These are the first chords new players learn and playing these songs first gives them confidence.

Then, as we get more difficult, the experienced players get a chance to feel challenged.

Finally, I introduce new songs to the group each week because I get bored easily! More seriously, I think everyone gets bored if they have to play the same songs each week, week after week for years.

Here is how Gillian Altieri from the San Jose Ukulele Club (http://sanjoseukeclub.org) chooses their songs:

> *Genre-wise, anything goes as long as the song isn't too complex. I avoid songs with gratuitous half-step key changes. Too many chord diagrams on too many song sheets and you'll have folks walking out. A lot of guitar songs are written in the key of E, which a lot of uke players shy away from so sometimes (not always) I will of transpose the song into an easier key. I usually go down, like to D or C so if folks want to play in the original key at home, they can use a capo. At the meetings, I try to have a comfortable mix of easy, intermediate and challenging songs. I have been told the word is out that if you want to play easy songs all the time, go to (nameless) uke club. If you want to learn something and/or improve your own playing skills, go to the SJUC club.*

During our first year, we lost a few members because we repeated the same songs week to week and didn't mix things up enough. I took their feedback seriously and tried to create a program in a way that captures everyone's interest. The jam session at the end lets members take the stage.

We play 10-12 songs during the jam session, and often repeat songs that had clunky parts. (See the Format section of this book) This gives novice players a chance to gain confidence and the experienced players a chance to try to chord voicings or solos.

When to Get 'Off Book'

Have you ever seen a jam session with other players who they just know what chords to play at just the right time with no music in front of them? There's not secret in being able to do that. Every song has a pattern of chords and the relationship between those chords is static. Basically, it's a pattern that can be transposed to any key. Picture this, the song is going strong, everyone is grooving, moving, playing, each person takes a solo. They make eye contact and the next guy or gal jumps in. Every note they play in the solo sounds super. It can be exhilarating to watch and even more fun to join in.

They can do this because they understand how to play by ear. They can hear the relationships between the chords, find the key and pickup on the pattern those chords appear. It might sound like a lot going on there, but with a little practice anyone can learn this. I asked Jim D'Ville, a music educator and facilitator who is on a mission to get ukulele players off the paper and playing music by ear, to share his thoughts on getting off the book.

Teach the songs in your group in a musical fashion. That means, at first, not using sheet music handouts. If people are reading off a piece of paper they are not fully engaged in the act of listening, they are multi-tasking, i.e reading, strumming, singing, etc. Tell the group the key of the song and the chord progression. Have the group sing the root note of the key (as stated below). Count it off and play it for the group so they get the sound of it in their ears. Start with fun I-V7-I (C-G7-C) songs like Jambalaya or Take Me Back To Tulsa. Most people already know how these tunes go and can sing the chorus without looking at any music.

All jams run smoother when the players use the number system to call out chords. The key you choose to play the song is assigned the number 1. All the other notes of the scale are numbered in order. In the key of C it would look like this. C=I, D=II, E=III, F=IV, G=V, A=VI, B=VII. In the key of Ab, for example, it's much easier for the jam leader to call out "I-V-I" than to call out the letters "Ab-Eb-Ab." By getting used to using the numbers instead of the letters you'll also have a much easier time transposing songs to other keys.

One reason people develop a reliance on using sheet music is they are not taught how to listen for the chord changes to simple songs. With a little ear-training most everyone can hear the I-V7-I relationship. Collect as many fun and familiar songs that use this song form to bolster your jam song repertoire. Genres to search for easy two-chord songs include rock, pop, folk, old time, bluegrass, and reggae.

Song Resources

Here's a list of places I go to find new songs for the group. There are plenty more out there, so consider this a jump start. The websites listed here offer you instant access to thousands of songs and are quite sufficient for the first years of your group.

Karen Snair, a uke player in Canada, has a great suggestion for finding songs:

> *I know of a local ukulele club that uses the book titled: "The Daily Ukulele: 365 Songs for Better Living" by Jim Beloff and Liz. The book used to cost about $25 but it has gone up to about $40. (Canadian pricing) It's a bit expensive for some people but it contains enough songs to last one a long time. Every year, they add a few songs from this book to their repertoire. If you are considering this book, ask if people can afford it. Sometimes it's also available at the local library. If you know it's going to be used by your club a lot, you can also request that the library purchase it so that members can take it out. This enables members to take it out and do what they need to do.*

The simplest format is what's called a "song sheet" with chords above lyrics and chord diagrams clearly visible.

Song Resources

Giant list of song resources:

- Halifax Ukulele Songbook is a great place to start: https://halifaxukulelegang.wordpress.com/hug-songbook
- Richard G's Huge Song List: http://www.scorpexuke.com/ukulele-songs.html
- Ukester Brown: http://www.ukesterbrown.com/song-sheets.html
- Doctor Uke gives you the audio and chords: http://www.doctoruke.com/songs.html
- Ukulele Songs: http://www.ukulelesongs.com
- Got A Uke: http://www.gotaukulele.com
- Turlock Uke Jamz: http://www.turlockukejamz.org/songs.html
- Yo!Ukulele: http://yokulele.com/ukulele-song-sheets/
- Ukulele Hunt: http://ukulelehunt.com/blog/
- Chordie: http://www.chordie.com/topsongs.php?cat=Uke+Collections
- Hey Ukulele: http://www.heyukulele.com/free-content/
- Ukutabs: https://ukutabs.com/
- The Ukulele Teacher: https://www.youtube.com/user/TheUkuleleTeacher
- Cynthia Lin: http://www.tigardukes.com/cynthialin
- Got a Uke: http://www.gotaukulele.com
- Jim's Ukulele Songbook: http://ozbcoz.com/Songs/index.php

An Important Note on Copyright Law

This summer we were invited to play at the Grange with one caveat, that we only play public domain songs or songs written before 1922. When I inquired further, it turns out that an organization called BMI was going after The Grange for having violated copyright law. They told me that each Grange Hall would need to pay $1,200 for a blanket license to host performances that included any copyrighted song. Barring that, they would only be able to play public domain songs or songs older than 1923. This limitation would seriously hamper our set list!

Luckily, a few months before the concert they decided to pay for the blanket license and we were able to choose any song we wanted for the concert.

Most entertainment premises have a blanket license, so you are likely covered, however, you might be required to make a list of the music you perform.

When you are practicing in your jam session, you do not need to worry about licensing those songs as it is not considered a "performance" and falls under the Fair Use clause which you can read about here: https://copyright.columbia.edu/basics/fair-use.html

As long as your jam sessions remain non-commercial and are for educational purposes, you'll be ok.

An Important Note on Copyright Law

Gillian Altieri who runs the San Jose Ukulele Club (http://sanjoseukeclub.org) told me this about protecting her club from copyright issues:

> *I say in BIG letters that our song sheets are for educational purposes only. I don't want any trouble with the copyright police. I've been told that if we made a songbook, people would buy it. As soon as money is involved, even if the cost of the book just covers the cost of printing, I think we would be asking for trouble. I also filed paperwork with the State of California stating that our Club is a non-profit, unincorporated entity.*

As soon as you get on stage somewhere, you'll have to find out from the venue if they are covered with a blanket license. If the venue doesn't have a blanket license, you can either purchase one yourself for your club, or contact the license holders for each of the songs you wish to perform to acquire written permission.

TOOLS TO MANAGE YOUR UKULELE GROUP

Welcome to the digital age of music. You now have more choices than ever before. You can choose to manage your group manually or you can choose to leverage modern tools to help you save time. (Or you can be a slave to technology!)

Remember that when you save time, you lower the barriers to creating good habits, and when you have easy (well established) habits; your ukulele group has a better chance of survival.

An Important Note on Copyright Law

In my day job, I develop educational programs that show baby-boomers how to leverage modern technologies, like social media, to find gainful employment.

Both my mom and dad are baby boomers and both are extremely technical. My dad and I used to build computers when I was a kid. He is nearly 80 and still freelances in database design, search engine optimization and web development. My mom has picked up digital photography in her second act and spends hours using extremely complex software in post-production.

Despite these examples, I often hear from audience members I'm teaching, "I'm too old to use this kind of technology." Or, "I'm just not good with all this new stuff."

Let me say right off the bat that if this is the story you're telling yourself, you are making a choice to limit yourself and you are jeopardizing the success of your group. Baby boomers have lived through more technical change than any other generation, from AM radio, to color TV to microwaves in a single lifetime.

First off, your willingness to learn new software applications has nothing at all to do with your age, as the example of my parents illustrates. Secondly, what's more important, maintaining a self-defeating narrative about who you are, or creating an inspiring and long-lasting musical group that will survive and thrive beyond your manual control?

In the following chapter, I will introduce you to some of the most powerful technologies available, which will ensure your group's success. If you find yourself overwhelmed, simply take a break. But don't discount the options that I present here. Using them, however stumblingly, could be the difference between an ukulele group that thrives or one that fizzles out the second you get tired of making 150 "Xerox" copies each week.

Who knew this little book about starting an ukulele group would challenge you like this!

On a personal note, I love learning new things. It's why I picked up the uke in the first place. And it's a compulsion that leads me to explore many tools. Luckily for you, I've found a combination of essential technologies for the effective organizing of any musical jam group.

Use what you like, though I highly suggest trying all of them out. After all, the challenges I faced starting and maintaining TUG will likely be identical to the challenges you'll face starting and continuing your own group.

Finally, and as a side note, all of the applications and software tools in this chapter have extremely good support pages. YouTube offers thousands of help videos for pretty much anything you want. If you get stuck, be patient, and check out the support page and YouTube for self-serve help. If you're still stuck, send an email with your question to the respective application's customer service team. I've done this many times and have always found answers to my issues within 24 hours.

Onsong

If you're like me, you probably don't like paying for apps on your phone or tablet. Even if it's $0.99, I'll look for the free options first, even if there are ads.

When I say that Onsong was the best $20 app I ever purchased, I really mean, Onsong is the only app I ever spent that much money on. Without it, I don't think I would have continued running TUG. It has been the difference between either spending hours trying to organize and distribute our weekly song list, or spending 10 minutes building a set list and exporting it to Dropbox (I'll get to that in the next section).

Onsong is an extremely powerful song organizing and editing IOS app for your iPad. Right now (May 2017) there isn't an Android version, although I've been told it is coming out. I'm happy to give you this excuse to go out and buy an iPad! There are song managers for Android but from what I can tell, none of them are as powerful as Onsong.

Regarding the purchase of an iPad, as your group grows, you'll find yourself with hundreds of songs in the repertoire. That's an awfully thick binder! And sorting it, carrying it and trying to balance it on your music stand is not really practical. With an iPad, you can keep thousands of songs on it, and it will still only weigh 1.5 lbs.

You can purchase an iPad inexpensively by visiting the Apple refurbished marketplace http://www.tigardukes.com/ipad, and for a few hundred dollars have a perfectly good device central to managing your uke group.

Then go to the App Store and search for Onsong and buy it. Trust me.

Here is my weekly workflow using Onsong:

1) On Wednesday, create a new set list and set the date to that of our next jam. This date will become the name of the set list automatically.
2) Add 10-12 songs from my TUG Songbook. I'll talk about how to pick your songs in a later chapter.
3) Export the set list to a Dropbox folder, which I've shared with my mailing list called, "This Week's Songs."
4) Get to the jam on Sunday, open up my iPad and all the songs for the week are right there, in the right order, ready to be played.

In the next sections, I'll talk about how to distribute this Dropbox folder via Mailchimp.

Adding songs to the Onsong Library is extremely easy. Here is my workflow for that:

1) Import new songs from a Dropbox folder called, "Put New Songs Here". Sometimes, I'll spend a few minutes formatting the song on my computer to make it more compatible with Onsong.

2) Find ways to convert the song to the Onsong format if possible. This might be importing a new version of the song from Safari, importing a text file or seeing if Onsong can read the document. Worse case scenario, I keep the song in whatever format I found it in.

3) Make sure I note how the song starts and ends either in the Onsong format or as a sticky note.

Onsong comes with a Safari plugin so that if you're on a website like Ukutabs.com, Chordie.com or ultimate-guitar.com, you have to click, "Add to Onsong" and it will get imported for you.

The benefit to having songs in the Onsong format are huge. You can change the key. You can change the formatting. You can edit the song on the fly. You can project lyrics during performance. And you will save storage room on your device.

Some sites are better at giving you a song formatted for Onsong. For example, Richard G's song collection very easily imports to Onsong whereas Dr. Uke's songs, although very nicely formatted, don't gel well with Onsong's import feature.

Onsong has a huge library of support videos, which cover almost all of its features, certainly for all the features I just described.

There're plenty more you can do with this app, change fonts, colors, spacing, chord charts, add backing tracks etc. But those are frosting on the cake.

Mailchimp

Ever get a mass email from someone who put every other recipient's email address in the To or CC box? I have, and each time this happens I feel like my privacy has been violated. I didn't consent to have all those other people get my email address.

If you were planning on pasting people's email addresses into an email, please don't — even if you BCC the list. Here are three good reasons:

- It's considered spam. If you did that in Canada or to a Canadian, you'd pay a $12,000 fine. It's against the law. Isn't that good enough :)
- It looks extremely unprofessional and people won't take you seriously.
- It's a huge pain in the butt to manage an email list. Not only would copying and pasting your list be a waste of time, but you'd also have to manage bounced emails, unsubscribe requests and email address changes.

You'll save hours of time by simply signing up for a free Mailchimp account, which at the same time will help you avoid the legal consequences of mismanaging people's private information.

Go here to sign up: http://www.tigardukes.com/mailchimp [affiliate link]

Mailchimp is free for up to 2,000 people on your list. It's extremely user friendly and will easily integrate with your website to make recruiting a breeze.

Here is my weekly workflow in Mailchimp. It takes me 10 minutes to do this:

1) Duplicate last week's campaign (email), rename it and update the subject line.
2) Write up any important announcements
3) Update the song list from the Onsong set list I just created, see last section
4) Send the email

At that point, Mailchimp will automatically personalize the email with the recipient's first name, remove any bounced emails and allow people to unsubscribe on their own if they chose to.

With Mailchimp, you can customize your Please Confirm page and Thank You page. Add instructions to those pages:

Confirm page: You're almost done. Please click "confirm" in the email waiting for you.

Thank You page: Please join our Facebook group here (add link) and download our latest songs here (add link)

If you want to see how I've set things up, you can sign up for TUG here and then unsubscribe after you've checked it out: http://eepurl.com/cMDyb1

Here is the anatomy of a weekly email:

- Personalized first-name greeting
- Any important announcements like upcoming concerts or community events
- The Dropbox link to the "This Week's Songs" folder

- The song list
- Essential details, like the time and location of the jam, for any new subscribers

Here's an example email you are welcome to use as a template:

Hi Joshua,

Ok. There are some important updates for you.

Easy one first; This Friday (3/31), at Pacific Pointe Retirement Inn, we'll be playing at 6:30 pm. Feel free to come and watch!

Next, the Spring Garden Party at The Grange is now on May 6th (not April 2nd). This means we'll be meeting this Sunday for TUG! If you want to play in that concert, please let me know. It's on a Saturday morning from 11:15 to 11:45.

Songs for April 2nd

Access this Week's songs HERE
- *Bad Moon Rising*
- *L-O-V-E*
- *Enjoy Yourself*
- *Wind of Change*
- *In the Jailhouse Now*
- *Que Sera Sera*
- *I am Weary, Let me Rest*
- *Blue Skies*
- *White Sandy Beach*
- *Caroline (from the Old Crow Medicine Show)*

- *The Black Velvet Band*

The last 30 minutes of the jam are dedicated to you! Bring your own songs to present or share with the group.

The Basics

We are meeting this Sunday from 2-4 pm at the Winona Grange (address below).

Our songbooks can be found here:
http://tigardukes.com/songbook

Our Facebook Group is here:
https://www.facebook.com/groups/tigard.ukulele.group

Dropbox

We've covered how to manage your songs and how to communicate with your members. Now, let's talk about the best way to distribute the songs themselves.

The best and most secure way to do this is by signing up to Dropbox here: http://www.tigardukes.com/Dropbox [Affiliate link]

First, create a folder inside your main Dropbox folder with the name of your group. Ours is called, "TUG Songs".

Then create several subfolders, including the following:

- This Week's Songs
- Upload New Songs Here
- Song Library
- Design Elements

Using Dropbox, copy the Share Folder link for This Week's Songs and keep the URL in an easy to access place. You'll want to put it in your emails in Mailchimp and on your Website if you want to make your songs easy to find for members.

People DO NOT need to have a Dropbox account to access this folder. They click the link and the shared folder will open in their browser. Then they can download the song by clicking on the icon that looks like this:

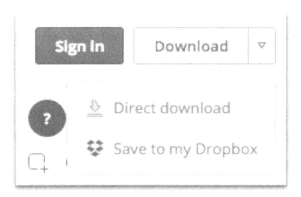

I think that Dropbox changes the link every 6-12 months. So be prepared to update your link every so often.

Dropbox is free for the first month then it's around $99/year.

Personally, I use Dropbox to backup and store all my files on the cloud. They have excellent encryption and, so far, have not had a single security breach. However, like any service on the cloud, you'll want to change your password every 6-12 months.

Also, some people will find that their browser doesn't properly print files. This problem happens when someone doesn't download the file first before printing. Some browsers will open the PDF in a new tab which could be impossible to print. Then have the person download the PDF first, then try to print it.

Facebook Private Group

If building community is one of your goals with starting a uke group, there's no better way to accelerate this than creating a Facebook Group.

Facebook has over 1 Billion users. And whether you like it or not, chances are that 90% of your members will be active on Facebook.

I created two communities on Facebook, a public Page and a private Group. I found that the private Group is way more active. People are posting in the TUG Group every day. They share videos, funny uke related images, or simply nice comments.

There are a few important admin details to remember with any Facebook private Group:

- You'll have to manually approve new members. If you forget, there will be no one there! Facebook will alert you when someone new knocks on the door.
- Members of the Group might not be on your mailing list. You can post instructions for signing up and Pin the post to the top so that new members will get your emails.
- If you don't model the behavior you want in the community, you might be disappointed. Remember to post frequently, and in your comments, set a supportive tone to encourage more posts.

Another cool feature with Facebook is the ability to create events. I don't create events for our weekly jam sessions, but I do for our community events and for our concerts. This allows members to easily invite their friends to join us. I've seen concert events get shared hundreds of times and we've always had great turnouts.

Having an active Facebook Group is a great way to keep up the momentum and energy from your jam session.

Those 10% of members who are not on Facebook probably abstain from it for privacy reasons. It's no surprise; Facebook uses our personal data to sell to advertisers, and probably to our governments as well. And for this reason, many people chose not to use it.

Be sensitive to the fact that some of your members will feel strongly opposed to using Facebook and will, therefore, miss out on many of the online discussions. So don't assume everyone in the live jam group will be savvy to what has been discussed online.

Website

Let me get right to the point. You need to create a website for your group and that website needs to look nice. Even if you are primarily focused on Meetup.com to promote and organize your group, you still need to have a website.

Here's why. With a website you can:

- Control your message and your branding
- Increase the ease with which new members can find you via Google
- Build your own mailing list, not one that Meetup.com owns
- And because this isn't the 1990s, your website needs to be more than an online brochure. In fact, with almost free options, your website can be a mecca for:
- Recruiting new members via SEO (see next section) and Mailchimp (see previous section)
- Sharing news and information via the blogging feature
- Creating online discussions with comments and social sharing
- A cathartic and rewarding sharing experience (I couldn't think of anything else, but I wanted to have a eighth bullet point!)

Here's the bad news. Creating a website, although essential to your group's success, is probably the biggest pain in the neck you'll have to deal with. There are more steps in this process and more potholes than anything else you will do to create your group.

Your options are to spend a weekend and work your way through my instructions here, learn a new skill and feel empowered. Or you could hire someone to set this up for you. Services like Fivver.com or Up-Work.com offer affordable tech support services.

I don't usually advocate using FourSquare or other online website building platforms because they tend to be more expensive than learning how to do this yourself and they don't offer the same flexibility as Wordpress. Sure, if you want to spend $200/year on a website, be my guest. But you'll still need to design your site, write the copy and learn a new platform. They do have nice templates and are simpler to set up and use. And that might be good enough value.

In these instructions, I'll show you how to spend 8-16 hours and $60/year.

Gill Wales, founder of one of my favorite websites Yo! Kulele (http://yokulele.com) said this about building her website:

> *My oldest son, a design student, has helped with the technical side of running the site and if you are not a website designer (which I am certainly not) you do need someone not only to talk through what you want your site to look like, but also to help you with the initial setting up and most importantly, with ongoing support through trouble shooting and updating. We used a template from 'Themeforest' in conjunction with 'Wordpress' which was easy for*

me to get my head round after some initial training. Please do NOT pay someone a fortune to build you a website. Try and find someone who can help you do it with simple programs from the internet at a fraction of the cost.

Below are step-by-step directions on how to build your website. Although each step is simple, it isn't necessarily easy. Businesses spend anywhere between $2,500 and- $25,000 for new websites. No one is expecting you to build the next Ukulele Underground or spend that kind of money. However, nice design and thought-through functionality will go a long way in building trust online.

Hosting

First, you need a place online to host or store your website. Hosting could cost around $4/month.

I use a very reliable and affordable hosting company called Site Ground for all of my websites. They have great support, reasonable rates, and very reliable services. Also, if you purchase your domain name with Site Ground they'll typically give you some free months off your hosting.

If you use my affiliate link, I get a couple of bucks, which helps me keep this book out there in the world.

Sign up for Site Ground here:

https://www.siteground.com/go/ukebook

During sign up you'll be asked to purchase a domain name. Try using your group's name with a .com, .net or .org suffix. When you use Site Ground to purchase your domain, you'll save a bunch of time and headache, plus they often have good bundle promotions.

The great thing is if you get stuck purchasing a domain and hosting, their website offers live chat support. Ask them to guide you.

Again, a little time, effort and patience could save you hundreds of dollars a year on your website.

Wordpress

Now that you have a domain name and a hosting account, you need to install Wordpress. Wordpress is the website platform that runs more than 80% of the Internet. It's incredibly flexible, easy to use and most importantly, free.

In Site Ground, log into the Cpanel area and install Wordpress on your domain. You'll have to pick a username and password for your admin account. Be sure to pick something secure and something you'll remember. That way, you won't feel any barrier to signing in often.

Site Ground has some very clear step-by-step tutorials on installing Wordpress. You can find them here:

https://www.siteground.com/tutorials/wordpress

The Divi Theme

Plain old Wordpress doesn't look that interesting. Plus it's not that easy to make design changes without knowing the CSS coding language. So you'll want to install a theme.

Themes change the look and feel of your Wordpress site without changing the content.

While there are thousands, if not millions of free themes available, the theme I like to use is called Divi.

You can purchase Divi here: http://www.tigardukes.com/divi [Affiliate Link]

This one-time purchase will make building your site so easy!

Once downloaded, go to your Wordpress site, click on Appearance, and then upload new theme.

Now you can create new pages and posts, use the Divi Editor for layout design, load built-in templates and use the on-page editor to design your new website. Plus there are a ton of helper videos on YouTube for using Divi.

When you set up Divi, you can connect your Mailchimp account in the settings area. When you do this, you'll be able to use Divi's built-in Newsletter sign-up module to start recruiting new members.

This is my favorite part of building sites. You get to choose layouts, colors, font sizes, backgrounds etc.

Find 3-5 websites you like then model your site based on those designs. Practice designing your site, publishing it, and then making the changes you want.

The essential pages you'll want to build are:

- **Home**, include your newsletter opt-in form
- **Contact us**, your phone number and group's location
- **Song list**, include that Dropbox link to your songs here
- **News** or Blog where you can post photos, videos, articles, guidelines and news. The more content you post, the higher your site will rank on Google.

SEO Basics

Search Engine Optimization, or SEO, includes techniques for getting your website to rank on Google for certain keywords.

This is by far the most valuable and (sometimes) the most tedious thing you can do to grow your group. Whenever new people show up to TUG I always ask them, "How did you hear about us?"

And most of the time their answer is, "I found you on Google." Guess what? That's because I optimized my site to make it easy for Google. That's all SEO is.

I'm glad I optimized my site right away. But it wasn't exactly the most glamorous work. Do it once and then enjoy the benefits later.

With good SEO, we grew from seven people in my living room to 30 people in a large Grange hall and 150 on my mailing list.

Even though there are countless books, courses and blogs on this topic, I think I can break it down for you in a simple and actionable way so that you can grow your group too.

Remember that the goal of SEO work is to get your website to show up when someone googles: *Your Location + ukulele*. Therefore, you are only really concerned with one keyphrase.

To make this simple, write down your keyphrase here:

Your location is: _____

Your group is called a (circle one): Club, Group, Association, *other:*
_____

There you go. If my keyphrase is Tigard Ukulele Group, then yours is:
_____

SEO has two categories, internal optimization and external optimization. Put aside an hour, log into your Wordpress site and let's do this!

External Optimization

Unless there are other ukulele groups in your area it will be fairly easy to rank your website without much external optimization. I'm assuming yours is the first group.: If that's not your case it will be much harder to rank, but not impossible. You might add what makes your group different, like "weekly" or "for beginners" to your on-page keywords. Be patient, follow these steps and wait for Google to do its thing.

External Optimization refers to the number and quality of the links that refer back to your website. The more links to your site from external sources, the better. Here are the main external links you should strive for:

- Other area ukulele groups: ask the webmaster of those sites to link back to you. TUG is listed on the Portland Ukulele Association website, for instance. Refer to my Partnerships chapter for more on getting these kinds of links.
- Ukulele Magazine's directory of ukulele groups: go to this page and submit your site to be included http://www.ukulelemag.com/club-hub. They will have the link up in a day or two.
- Email GotAUkulele.com, a top 100 ukulele website to get your group listed here: http://www.gotaukulele.com/p/ukulele-clubs-and-societies.html
- Email Ukulele Hunt Directory here: http://ukulelehunt.com/2010/03/10/ukulele-clubs-and-groups/

- Your local newspaper: using the techniques you will learn in the Twitter section to get local news coverage, getting even one link from a newspaper will help boost your site rankings to page one.
- When you ask for backlinks, it's always best that the link is on your keyphrase. In other words:
- Avoid getting links that are "*http://*" exposed on a webpage
- Avoid generic keywords that are linked to you, like the word "ukulele"
- The best links will include your group name, location and the word "ukulele", such as "Tigard Ukulele group"

Internal Optimization

Internal Optimization refers to the steps you can take on your own website to help Google make sense of it.

Luckily Divi and Wordpress make this process extremely easy.

The first step is to install a plugin called Wordpress SEO by Yoast. This plugin will do most of the heavy lifting for you including creating a Robots.txt and Sitemap.xml. If that's Greek to you, don't worry about it. The plugin will do it for you. Smile.

Here are the steps you will need to take manually to make sure you have excellent on-site optimization:

1) Make sure your website is searchable: head to your Wordpress settings area, click on Reading and make sure search engines can index your site.
2) Take a look at your Divi Theme Settings and update your site's Title, and Subtitle with your keyphrase present.
3) Go to the Edit area for each of the new pages you created. Below the Divi edit area you'll now see the Wordpress SEO settings box. Give each page a different Title and Description which include your location (Tigard) and the words Ukulele or Uke, and club or group.
4) Include a Description for very image you use
5) On the page itself, make sure your written content has keywords, which include your location, "ukulele", and group or club.
6) Post a couple of blog posts. The more content you have the better Google will like you. Posts can be news, such as, "We're starting a new Uke Club in town".
7) Find ways to link to other pages on your site from within other pages. This is called *internal linking*. A fast way to do that is to refer to the News (blog) section from your home page and have Blog posts refer to the Contact page "for more details."
8) Install a plugin called Divi Custom Footer, and add the name of your group, the address and phone number in your footer. This way, every page will have the most important details.

This work will take 1-2 hours, but will pay dividends later.

Tools Summary

You may have noticed that I really nerded out in this chapter. I do love my toys!

For those of you less prone to using technology, let me summarize the tools I use for TUG.

- **Onsong** to organize our songs and build set lists that can be exported to Dropbox
- **Dropbox** for the distribution of the songs to a large group of people
- **Mailchimp** to manage my email list and communications
- **Facebook Private Groups** to stay top-of-mind in between live sessions and build community
- **Wordpress** the platform for my website using the Divi theme and to get it SEO optimized

ORGANIZING YOUR FIRST MEETING

You have a vision. You have your tools. Now you need to figure out where you're going to meet, how you're going to lead people in songs, or even where you're going to find new songs. I'll go into detail in this next chapter to help you kick off your first jam session with a boom or a strum!

Finding a Venue

Finding a venue was the hardest part of starting The Tigard Ukulele Group (TUG). We had outgrown my living room in months and were propelled quickly into looking for community centers. Boy, did I learn about that!

First of all, you might not be comfortable inviting total strangers to your house; your living room may be extremely limited in capacity and not a sustainable option for a growing group.

We started with seven people in our living room. When we got to 15, we started our scramble for a better venue. It's ok to start there, but don't make our mistake. Start your search for a bigger space right away.

In the UK, many uke clubs meet in pubs. In a way, this is ideal. You have drinks and food readily available. People are naturally more relaxed. And there's an expectation that the jam session is more of a party than a performance.

For us, this wasn't possible. I remember when I called a local pub and the conversation went like this:

> *"Fanno Creek Pub, how can I help you?"*

> *"Hi there, who can I talk to about using the community meeting space in the back of your hall?"*

"That'd be me. I'm the manager."

"Ok, well, we have an ukulele group and we're looking for a place to hold our weekly jam sessions."

"You're joking, right?"

"No."

-Click-

I had similar conversations at locally owned cafes, most of whom were willing to take my money, but wouldn't commit to a regularly scheduled event, and were on the fence about letting a musical group in.

We tried meeting at a Whole Foods. The one near us has a test kitchen that went mostly unused. The acoustics were terrible and the seating was, well, kitcheny.

Finally, I contacted my local Grange. They were open to having us. Not only would they not charge us, they wanted us to play at their annual Garden Party. In exchange, I had to become a Grange member so that their insurance would cover the group and we would provide some portion of our donations to them. In fact, I give them the whole jar. I don't want to deal with the money!

If you aren't familiar with what a Grange is, the Grange is a 100+ year old fraternal organization centered on agriculture and the culture of farmers in America. In our town, we no longer have much agriculture, but we still have square dancing, Irish music, puzzle exchanges and garden parties with free seeds. Most Grange buildings come performance-ready, with a stage, hardwood floors and lots of chairs.

Another good option for your group is the local library. My library is so under budget that they don't let anyone use their community room. But the town next door has a library willing to host an ukulele group.

Finally, a great option for your group is the local community center, a YMCA, JCC or an area community center. Chances are they won't charge you for the use of their room. Plus, they'll help you get the word out about your group. These centers thrive when members of the area show up and get involved. They often have budgets ready to spend to do this so you're making their job easier, too.

The most important thing to consider when selecting a venue is the vibe. Where people play music will influence how they see your group and how they feel about the music they're making. Pick a location that reflects who and what your group is all about.

Setting the Tone

I've been to ukulele groups that didn't feel very friendly. The people sitting next to me wouldn't talk to me. The songs went by very quickly and with very little instruction. My neighbors made faces at me for being such a beginner (or at least I imagined their fangs out when I played a C6 the whole time). I spoke with other beginners after that session who felt similarly. None of us went back.

That's not what the ukulele is all about!

When I started TUG, I knew my group was going to reflect the spirit of Aloha as much as possible. To me Aloha means:

- Friendly
- Supportive
- Fun
- Welcoming
- Community

You'll have members come to your group who are very experienced, and you'll have new players who are, scared, apologizing for messing up and feeling intimidated.

I make it a point to always honor these new players by repeating, "It's ok. We're all here to have fun. You'll do great! I'm so glad you're here."

"I only know two chords."

"It's ok. We're all here to have fun. You'll do great! I'm so glad you're here."

"I've only been playing for a month."

"It's ok. We're all here to have fun. You'll do great! I'm so glad you're here."

"I've never been to an ukulele group before."

"It's ok. We're all here to have fun. You'll do great! I'm so glad you're here."

"Can I bring my guitar next time?"

"Heck no!" (Just kidding, we welcome all instruments! We even have a flautist.)

Soon even our experienced players are saying it. As our group grew and new folks would sit next to experience players, I'd overhear them saying, "Its ok. We're all here to have fun. You'll do great! I'm so glad you're here."

My heart burned with pride! Yay Team Aloha!

One member, Tony, came to TUG a year ago, after his granddaughter gave him an ukulele as a retirement gift. He showed up at our group a week later knowing absolutely nothing. Tony is an army veteran, and very active in his retirement, participating in other hobbies like woodcarving and photography. He's actually a national champion American Mahjong player.

We welcomed him. I had him sit next to me on his good side so he could hear me (he wears a hearing aid) and made sure to ask him if we'd see him again next week. He said yes.

Each week he apologized for not practicing. "It's ok. We're all here to have fun. You'll do great! I'm so glad you're here."

A year later, Tony is playing at all of our concerts and is our designated photographer for all of our community parties. He takes great pictures too!

So, set your heart in Aloha and bring a friendly, fun and supportive vibe to your group. As the leader, people will follow you.

I asked Bob Guz and Jen Richardson who co-founded the Austin Ukulele Society (*http://austinukulelesociety.com*) in 2011 about how they set the tone of their group. The AUS has been a go-to resource for me on YouTube for some great group playing. This is what Bob said:

> *Before the first meeting of your group, it's important to define your group's purpose and goals. Is your group intended to be a place for beginners to learn the basics, or more about providing seasoned players a venue to jam together? Are you focused on a particular style, genre, or period of music, or is your plan to cast a wide net to attract musical tastes of all kinds? Do you plan to provide organized lessons for attendees to improve their skills, or will the meetings be more "free-form", with participants sharing tips on an ad-hoc basis? Will you be concentrating on instrumental tunes, or are your meetings going to be sing-a-longs as well as strum-a-longs? The answers to these questions will in turn drive the agendas of your meetings.*
>
> *For example, one of the Austin Ukulele Society's (AUS) key goals is to eliminate as many barriers to participation as possible. We charge no meeting dues (funding our operations through the sale of AUS t-shirts), and impose no limits on experience level. Our target*

audience is adults (although children are welcome to attend with their parents) and we have been very successful in attracting participants from their 20s through their 80s by deliberately choosing songs from multiple genres, styles, and decades. The format of our meetings is definitely patterned as an educational workshop.

Regardless of your group's goals and objectives, it is important to have one individual designated as the meeting "leader" or "facilitator." The role of the group leader is to provide instruction and encouragement, keep the group focused, and prevent more "outgoing" individuals from dominating the proceedings. In general, this helps promote a positive experience for everyone in attendance.

Gillian Altieri from the San Jose Ukulele Club (http://sanjoseukeclub.org) has a very different approach than I do. Where TUG sits in a circle and I raise my hand to get everyone's attention, SJUC uses a microphone to keep things under control.

Get a microphone so you can be heard and get people's attention. I'm not being condescending when I say you have to take charge like a kindergarten teacher does. The laughter and chatter is a good sign that people are having fun but sometimes a loud "Ahem" into the mic is needed.

Jam Agenda

Your group should run the same way each time. People like routines. Your brain works less when you follow routines and don't have to make so many decisions so run your group through the same agenda each time. When you make changes, make them small.

In fact, I didn't even know I did this. But when I asked long-time player Matt to lead the group one Sunday when I was away on business, he reflected my agenda back to me. I'm glad he was paying attention.

Before we start playing songs I follow this flow:

1) Introduce new members and go around the circle with names and something to share
2) Remind people we need participants for any upcoming performances
3) Remind people to contribute a few bucks to keep the lights on (also at the end)
4) Poll the crowd for the number of walk-in songs we have for the open mic at the end
5) "Let me know if you have other announcements you'd like to make." Sometimes there are up-coming uke related events, lost and found, or news that players want to talk about

After announcements, we launch into our song list for the day. This goes for about an hour and a half, depending on how many walk-in songs we have.

Jam Agenda

Walk-in songs are saved to the end of the meeting where I dedicate the last 30 minutes to an open mic. Over the years, I've found that people really love sharing their own songs either to play with the group, or as a solo.

This is a great way for you, the group leader, to discover new songs to add to the regular songbook. Often someone will bring a walk-in song that everyone loves. I make note of those and add them to a list to play later.

When people bring songs for the group to play, I ask them to bring 15-20 copies, and if possible, send me a digital version for OnSong. (See the Tools section.)

Here's our 2-hour agenda

1) Announcements and introductions (5-10 min)
2) Jam session (~1.5 hours)
3) Walk-in songs (~30 minutes)
4) Thank you for coming and see you next week!

What's your jam agenda?

Though I spend just 30 minutes to prepare for our weekly meetings Jen Richardson and Bob Guz from the Austin Ukulele society spend hours getting it just right. Here's what Bob said about their agenda:

> *Preparing for a ukulele group meeting requires a great deal of preparation. I would estimate that each hour of meeting time requires about 3-4 hours of prep time, perhaps more. Know in advance*

which songs you plan to work on, what techniques or skills you are going to cover, and who will be responsible for each part of the meeting.

Playing music as part of a group can be an intimidating experience, especially for those new to it. To help ease these anxieties, it is very helpful to let folks know right from the get-go what they can expect. Let people know in advance which song or songs you plan to play, walk through the agenda when the meeting kicks off, and publish photos and videos afterwards so that people thinking of coming in the future get a sense of what the meetings are like.

I asked The Ukulele Dude, Mark Swarthout, who is a charter member of Motor City Ukes, which has meet monthly for seven years in Farmington, Michigan, the Great Uke State, what his jam agenda is. You can learn more about Mark here: http://www.theukuleledude.com. Here is what Mark said:

At Motor City Ukes, we have a general format we follow each month. A quick introduction of first name and where we are from around the room and we have our first strum session. Then we have general announcements related to ukulele programs and events in the area and discussion of possible gigs. This feeds into open mic time and the month's program, a 20-minute time slot for musical education.

Our programs have included a drum circle, introduction to harmonica, Nashville notation, GHS String presentation by the GHS rep, song writing, and Hawaiian Vamps. Everyone with musical knowledge is encouraged to share their knowledge! We plan one meeting a year that is specifically aimed at beginners and we have an annual swap meet to buy, sell, and exchange ukulele and music items, but is also open for anything else you care to tout! This is followed by more strumming. The total time is just under 3 hours, including about half hour before and after for socializing.

Each month we chose a topic for the following month's meeting. It is often associated with a holiday that falls shortly after the meeting or the season. December is obviously holiday songs, March is Irish and October is Spooky/Ghostly or Halloween. Other themes have included colors, cars, love songs, travelling, beach, weather, drinking songs, kazoo, and even other countries.

Members then have a month to post songs on the topic for the group to do together. The rule is, if you post the song, you have to be ready to lead it! That includes review of the chords used and how to read the particular version. If we don't have enough songs to fill in the strumming time, we pull up an online song book on the projector and skim the table of contents until someone says "Let's do that one!" Again, if you call it out, you have to lead it! About half to two thirds of the meeting are strumming along.

Staying Together

Keeping together is by far, the most important consideration for playing satisfying music in your ukulele group.

Consider the very likely possibility that most of your members will never have been formally trained in music. That before picking up the uke, the most musical thing they did was sing in the shower. Of course, there's nothing wrong with this and you should welcome everyone! But it does present some issues musically.

Specifically, for most of your players, your jam session is likely the only group playing experience they have had with their uke. For the most part, their uke playing will be at home alone. At home, alone, if they get stuck on a song, they stop. If they speed up, no one is there to slow them down.

A music teacher told me once, "You can't get off the train; the train keeps on a goin'"

In other words, with a group, the momentum of the song is larger than each individual player. But when people don't listen, they find they've fallen off the train.

The problem is that if everyone gets off the train at once, the song falls apart. As a trained drummer, this drives me crazy. Some people are speeding up, others slowing down, others stop playing and look around. There I am with my eyes squeezed shut trying to keep the backbeat despite all of it.

When I was playing the drums and practicing hours a day back in college, the most helpful thing for me to do was play with a metronome. The click-click-click gave me something to hold onto. In other words, a backbeat.

Backbeats are an incredible musical tool. It originated from African music and continues to influence many pop songs to this day. Early jazz used backbeats to keep their highly syncopated rhythms danceable. Drummers called it, "Four on the floor" because the bass drum (the floor) hit all the quarter notes. Backbeats kept big bands together. They propel dance clubs into whirling ecstatic parties long into the night.

What TUG needed was a backbeat. Something everyone could hear so that they could reference the pace and cadence of the song; a reminder that the train keeps going.

That's where The Suitcase Drum idea came from.

After scouring YouTube for awhile, I came across this video:

All I needed to do was buy a $25 old suitcase on craigslist, get some Velcro, some old license plates and a couple of used drum pedals. The whole rig cost me less than $100 and took an hour or so to build.

Here's an image of my suitcase drum: https://youtu.be/ZpVj01gQza0

Figure 1: Joshua's Suitcase Drum

Regarding the coordination of playing both the uke and the drum, it came naturally to me. I think with some practice you can get it easily as well. If you tap your feet when you play, it's no different. With the drum, you're tapping your feet on a drum pedal. The physics of it is simple though you may need to get used to the feel of it at home first before you take it to your group.

A more conventional approach to bringing in a backbeat to your group is to have a bass player join you. It doesn't matter if the bass player plays a u-bass, upright bass or electric bass. The deep sound of the bass can be heard over even a hundred strumming ukes. Not only is it heard, but it's also felt in the chest. It's the key to keeping a group of any size together and at the right tempo.

Having a bass player versus not having a bass player is like night and day. I found our TUG bass player by attending a local jam session (all instruments), which I found on Meetup.com. There she was, after months of searching, playing the u-bass in a dark dusty bar with 20 guitarists, 2 fiddlers, 3 ukulele players, 2 flautists, and 4 mandolins.

When Bev is not at a TUG session, I notice it musically. I highly encourage you to make every attempt to get yourself a bass player.

Make sure they sit where they can see your fingers. This helps them keep the beat and know what chords you're playing.

Another thing, beware the egg shaker, tambourine or cowbell. What more cowbell?

If someone who is rhythmically challenged and gets hold of one of these awesome, song-wrecking weapons, disarm them immediately.

So to summarize, find a way to keep a backbeat. Whether it's doing it yourself with a simple drum or stamp box, or bringing in a bass player, the key to playing great music is staying together.

How to Lead Others

I frequently let others lead the group. I might be away traveling or looking for a Sunday off. Each time I delegate this, inevitably, the person tells me how hard it was. I don't feel it to be hard personally. Perhaps it's because I slowly learned the skill of leading others over the course of two years as the group grew. Therefore, it's a bit of a challenge for me to articulate exactly how to lead songs.

I asked a recent co-leader, Matt, to share his thoughts on what it was like during his leading experience.

Here's Matt:

> *Without prior musical experience, I started playing ukulele a bit over a year ago. Practicing alone was not very motivating, so I looked for uke groups I could join. I found The Tigard Ukulele Group (TUG) online, and stopped by one of their weekly jam sessions. The group was welcoming and fun and I found myself moti-*

vated to practice and improve my playing in order to better participate.

One day when Joshua asked me to fill in while he was away on a business trip, I hesitated. A litany of reasons to decline jumped to mind:

I'm busy.

I'm not a musician.

I can't sing well.

I don't have rhythm.

One thing I figured out quickly is that a music group gives back what you put into it. When individuals show up with positive energy and have a spirit of fun, it elevates the whole group experience. I embraced a "say yes" attitude with the group. Need help setting up chairs? Yes! Searching for volunteers to play at a concert? Yes! Need a co-leader to step in...ok, I'll say "Yes."

My time leading the group went well, and I still had fun!

If you decide to lead a uke song circle, here is my advice how to make each song run smoothly:

- *Hear the song in your head before you start counting, that might mean listening to it the day before to get it stuck in your brain*

- *Practice with a metronome at home to get better at keeping rhythm*

- *Describe any pickup notes and how to count around those, pickup notes are confusing for some people, this is where the song starts before the first beat. Think of the song "Hanalei by Moonlight", the lyric When you see" happens before the first beat,". So, you might count this song with "1,2,3,4,1,2 When you see..."*

- *Count into the song loudly, and be sure to play the first note and sing the first word, after that, look around the room and make sure everyone is having fun*

When announcing the song, you are about to play, consider telling a brief story about the song's history, or share what the song means to you, or make a comment about the composer. This can help connect the player to the piece of music in another way. Joshua has a way of punning us from one song to the next.

Note the key and time signature of the upcoming song. This is particularly important for songs in 3/4 or other non-common time, as the group can come apart quickly if everyone isn't on the same beat.

Provide a suggested strum pattern and tempo to the group. For instance, you might state the tune sounds good with a boom-chuka strum and a fast tempo in double time. Demonstrate a couple of lines for the group.

If a song presents an opportunity for an instrumental solo, be sure to ask for volunteers before the song starts. If nobody raises their hand, consider skipping the solo, but clearly explain that is the plan. We have players who enjoy playing a kazoo or harmonica during the solo portion of songs.

If not explicitly written on the sheet music, describe the introduction you plan to use to get into the song. If you as a leader aren't confident in the introduction, consider asking the group how they suggest starting the song. If nobody has an idea, you might choose to either launch-in without an introduction, or vamp on a chord until everyone is together, then count in the song start.

Note anything unusual about the ending. Often the hardest areas to keep a group playing well together are the start and ending of the tune. Will the song end on a tremolo or a single strum, or maybe a cha-cha-cha.

Point out any tricky chords or chord transitions that you noticed in your pre-review at home. Pay attention to facial expressions as you're talking. If people are frowning at their sheet music, ask if they have questions. Encourage discussion among the group regarding the best way to do tricky chords or transitions.

Don't feel bad about asking for opinions from the group. The role of the leader isn't to be the best musician, it is to organize the event and act as master of ceremony. Asking the group their thoughts on how to do something better is part of your role as leader.

Tap your foot loudly while counting off the start of the song to get everyone playing at the same tempo.

Launch the song!

If it crashes badly at some spot, it is OK to laugh and discuss what went wrong and how to fix it. Be patient.

Play through the song a second time if the tune has promise, but has a couple of rough spots that need repetition to get it right.

Smile even if you are stressed leading the group. People look to the group leader for more than tempo. If you are smiling and having fun, others will also.

Breathe a sigh of relief! You just helped spread joy in the world through sharing music.

Thanks Matt for these awesome insights!

The Whole Issue of Singing

I'm a terrible singer. I've taken lessons, done hours of voice training. It just doesn't come easy to me. If there's a song that needs a demo during a jam session, I usually volunteer Lily, my wife, to sing it; or another well tuned victim. As a natural consequence to my lack of melodic confidence, I've asked Jim D'Ville, author of the *Play Ukulele By Ear* DVD series and founder of the popular *Play Ukulele By Ear* website (www.PlayUkuleleByEar.com), to share some of his ideas on singing in your ukulele group.

> *If you want your ukulele group to sound good from the very first note, get the them in tune together. Have everyone tune-up their ukuleles, then have the group tune their ears and voices. I use an A-440 tuning fork to accomplish this (since the first string on the ukulele in C tuning is tuned to A). Strike the A fork on your knee and place it on your uke. Hum the resulting A tone. Get the group to join the hum fest. At this point you can introduce the concept of playing together in time. Strike the fork again, place it on your uke and count off 3-4-1 (4/4 time-four beats per measure). On the 1, get everyone to loudly sing: "AAAAAAAAAAA!" In a group setting, this usually comes out sounding pretty good.*
>
> *You have now introduced the concept of singing on pitch. Have you ever seen a barbershop quartet perform? Before each song starts the leader of the group states the key by blowing the root note on a chromatic pitch pipe. You can perform the same task at your group. Before each song, state the key of the song, play the tonic or root note of that key and have the group sing it. Repeating this procedure with each song will dramatically improve the over-all tonality of your jam.*

GETTING THE WORD OUT

The question is do you want to have more members? If so, how many more? What do you do if someone leaves and you want to fill their place?

As group leader, it's your job to market the group and get the word out. Don't worry, this part is really fun. In this chapter, we're going to cover social media promotion, building lasting partnerships and more.

Social Media

Love or hate it, social media is the best tool for spreading the word about your uke club. Remember, these are all tools used to accomplish a specific goal. The success of your group is bigger than you. It will bring joy to the lives of hundreds of people. Are you willing to do what it takes to make it succeed?

If you answer "yes", then please learn how to use Facebook and Twitter to promote your group. If you don't do this, be prepared to take years to get to where you want to be.

I made a promise to you in this book, and that was to show you everything I know about starting and growing a successful ukulele club. If you've made it this far, you can certainly handle the next two sections.

Facebook Ads

I took my mailing list from 50 to 130 in seven days and almost doubled our attendance with $100 and a Facebook ad campaign. It was an experiment that went very well. In fact, many of our early members came from that ad campaign. I stopped doing it because we'd already reached a size I liked and I didn't want any more members. There's no doubt that if I'd continued advertising on Facebook, we'd be 100 people a week.

This section will be fairly technical. Know that Facebook changes things frequently and if something I've told you here doesn't seem to make sense, chances are that the interface or functionality has changed. So, head on over to YouTube or Facebook to get an update.

Remember that Facebook ads require that you have already set up a group or page for your uke club first.

Facebook ads are highly targeted posts where you control the demographics, psychographics and social-graphics of who sees them based on conversions in your mailing list. You've probably seen posts in your Facebook timeline with the words "Featured Post" in the title. Well, someone made the image and paid for the ad so that someone like you could see it.

Head on over to Facebook.com/ads to get started:

1) Start a new campaign in the ads manager: https://www.facebook.com/ads/manager by clicking on the green Create Ad button
2) Enter the Campaign name. This name is only for your reference
3) Set your objective to Conversions, since you want Facebook to optimize the display of your ads based on people signing up to your newsletter
4) Name your ad set to your location. For example, I called one "Tigard" and another "Portland". Your campaign can have multiple ad sets, perhaps one for each of the surrounding towns

5) The conversion event is Lead, so when someone gets to the Thank You page for your email newsletter, that's a conversion because they've come a lead
6) Install the Lead Pixel code onto your Thank You page so that Facebook will be alerted when someone signs up. This might mean you create a new page on your Wordpress site called Thank You so that you can install this Pixel Code. Then program Mailchimp to send people to this custom page after they've signed up.
7) Set the location to your town, in other ad sets include the surrounding areas as well to match the name of the ad set
8) Set the Detailed Targeting to Interests, and of course, interested in Ukulele.

On the right, you'll see how big your potential audience will be. My Estimated Daily Reach was between 1,000 - 3,000 people; if yours is much bigger or much smaller than this range, play around with the location and interest settings.

This is the image I used:

I set a $20/day budget over the next 7 days and watched as my mailing list doubled. People were sharing my sponsored post, commenting on it and clicking the call to action.

This YouTube video is a very useful tutorial for getting started with Facebook ads: https://youtu.be/RGJnLHMkkik

Twitter

Every reporter uses Twitter. And especially, your local reporters monitor Twitter for news items.

Twitter is basically a steady stream of short messages, which can be searched. Reporters set up continuous searches with Twitter so that as soon as someone says the word, "Tigard" or "#Tigard" they'll know about it. If it's a topic they find interesting, they will DM or Direct Message you, which, is private, or they'll @message you, which is public.

If that sounds like a whole lot going on, well, it is!

The most important thing to know is that when you set up a Twitter account and start posting Tweets with your town's name, the local press notices.

This is exactly what happened with TUG.

I sent the following tweet from my personal Twitter account:

 @TigardOR I'm looking for a venue in **Tigard** for my new Ukulele Jam Group to practice. There's about 10-15 of us. Any suggestions?
31 Aug15 @JoshuaWaldman Joshua Waldman

That's all. It was me asking the city for suggestions on a venue for our group.

In a couple of days, I got a reply from Geoff, a reporter from the Tigard Times. He wanted to come to one of our sessions with a photographer for an article.

We exchanged phone numbers and set the whole thing up. In a month, this article came out: http://www.tigardukes.com/article

Do I particularly like Twitter? Not really. But I'm sure glad I use it, because that article attracted our next ten members.

I'm not going to go into how to set up an account in this book because there are so many other great resources out there, including books, YouTube videos and articles found on Google. All you need is a little curiosity and some patience to learn something new. The benefits of your time are very likely to be excellent coverage in your local newspaper.

Partnerships

Your ukulele club is part of a larger community. In your area, there are square dancing groups, salsa and swing dance clubs, puzzle exchanges, book groups, curling and who knows what else. All of these groups are looking for interested members to recruit. Some do it well while others remain small and obscure. Your uke club is one of many options.

After a few months of meeting in my living room, I decided I wanted more for my group. I printed up some posters and headed to my local music shop. I got to know the guys who work there, let them know about TUG, and asked if they would hang up my poster. They have a wall of ukuleles in the shop and whenever someone buys one, they let the customer know about our group.

Over the years, we've sent many of our members to their shop for repair services, accessories and new instruments. The shop is excited to promote us not just because they are passionate about music, but also, it makes good business sense. Plus, they're really nice people who want to help!

Now that your group is under way and you can deliver on your promise of a good time, consider reaching out to some of the music shops in your town.

Another great resource for spreading the word are local music teachers. Last winter, we invited an ukulele teacher to our group. He got to promote a new class he was starting to an instant audience of well-qualified potential students, and he got familiar with another local group to recommend to his other students. During his visit, I gave him some time to promote his business. He also taught us a new song and gave a sample lesson so everyone learned something new.

If you do ask a local ukulele teacher to come, be sure there's enough mutual value for them and your group. This is a great way to help your members find options to improve and help a (more than likely) struggling music teacher make a living doing what they love.

Once I had the website finished, I made sure to email the leaders of as many other local uke clubs as I could. Portland Ukulele Association

(PUA) for example has a whole webpage dedicated to Other Resources, teachers and other clubs in the area. They were more than happy to add a link to our group's website. The results of this have been fantastic.

In fact, many new members tell me that they found TUG because they enjoyed PUA but wanted something weekly or closer to their home. They went to the PUA website and there we were!

Many of our members attend more than one uke group. When they visit other clubs, they spread the word about TUG. As long as we keep being awesome, our member-ambassadors will spread the word for us.

There's no perfect group; there's only a good fit. Most groups recognize that their group might not be for everyone. Not all of the people who check out TUG want a weekly group that repeats songs a few times. Well, there are options for them and that's OK. Help those people who aren't a good fit find a group that's right for them. The other clubs will do the same.

Posters & Community

I'm not going to spend too much time on using posters for two reasons:

1) You know what it is-- you print up some posters and hang them around town.

2) As far as I can tell, they never did anything for our group.

Now that could be location specific and just where we live, I've noticed that even when cafes and restaurants have community boards, I've never seen anyone paying any attention to them. The one place I wanted to poster, where people pay attention, is the library. But they didn't put ours up for some reason. Probably a lot of other stuff going on and we are at the bottom of their list.

Here's what our poster looks like:

I paid a designer to do this because I'm not that good at graphic design. It only cost me $80. This could always be an option for you.

I put posters in:

- Cafes
- Music shops
- Pizza joints
- Super markets
- Community centers
- The library (but they didn't hang it!)

Perhaps you can think of ten more places your poster could go.

Remember this was the least effective way we got the word out.

Ok, that's it. Not one more word about that!

Meetup.com

Meetup.com is a website used to help a group of people interested in something stay organized and meet in person. It's the bridge between a virtual world and a physical world. There are Meetup groups about all kinds of things: software, hiking, Samoyed dogs. They are all local; enter your zip code and the thing you are interested in and chances are there's a group for you.

For example, I've attended Meetup events in Portland for urban hikes, bike rides, kayaking, jazz clubs, wine tasting and other things. Many ukulele clubs use Meetup to recruit new members, organize events and communicate with their members.

I chose not to use Meetup for TUG for a few reasons.

First, it costs $9.99/month and I don't want to pay a service for things I can do myself

Second, I didn't want to require money from my members. It should be optional and from the heart, and if I had $9.99 overhead, I'd ask members to help pay for it.

Third, I wanted to own the conversation. When you host via Meetup, Meetup owns the email address and stores all the conversations on their servers. It seems impersonal to me.

Fourth, I suspected that the ukulele demographic probably wouldn't turn to Meetup to find other players.

Now, for someone without much time and interest in doing all the stuff I outline in this book, Meetup might be a good solution, at least at first.

Instead of spending hours building a website, setting up Facebook ads, signing up for Mailchimp etc. all you need to do is get one Meetup account and pay $9.99.

It's a great solution if (1) you're getting started with your group and (2) you REALLY don't like technology and (3) you have very little time to put into your new club.

Finally, from what I can tell, the largest Meetup ukulele groups in Portland only have 8 players. I strongly suspect that if I had used Meetup for our group, we'd still be 10 people in my living room.

However, it could have gotten us started much faster. Though I'm sure I would have grown out of it soon enough.

Again, this comes back to your goals. If you want a super small group of people in your living room to jam and not have to spend much time organizing things, give Meetup a try.

KEEPING UP THE MOMENTUM

My biggest fear for TUG is that I'll get bored or overwhelmed or move away and stop running it, and then the group will die. After all the work I've put into it and all the lives we've touched that would really be terrible. In this chapter, we'll cover ways to make running the group easier so you don't burn out and how to ensure the group survives after you're ready to move on.

Habits & Checklists

Before checklists became popular, doctors would use their intuition to determine heart attack risk, running through a series of symptoms in their head. What Atul Gawande, author of The Checklist Manifesto (http://amzn.to/2oGdYvT), observed is that when doctors started using checklists during diagnostics, heart attacks in patients went down dramatically. According to his research this was both because of and despite their expertise. He notes that one reason is that we often skip steps after we become comfortable with a process. Also, there's something called, "decision fatigue" which happens when your brain stops being able to make choices when it's tired. Both of these situations can lead to bad outcomes.

Record the steps it takes you to organize and plan your group. Each week, follow that document and make adjustments to it as you learn new and better ways of doing things.

When I sit down to organize TUG every week, I'm not re-inventing the wheel. I follow the same steps each time, which takes a huge burden off of my shoulders. By following my steps, I don't have to struggle with new decisions. And this makes it a lot easier and faster.

In my calendar, I have an event set to repeat each week to remind me to "send out ukulele songs." Inside that calendar event, I have my checklist:

- Import or format any new songs for the week in Onsong

- Make new set list in Onsong
- Summarize any important announcements for the week in Mailchimp
- Put new set list in Mailchimp
- Send email

Because I'm constantly importing new songs that members send me, I'm never scrambling to find new songs to play each week. And because we have so many old songs, there's always material to review and revisit.

Documenting your own process might feel like a schlep at first. Sure, it takes you longer the first time to write down everything you do while organizing your group. However, the next week, when you go to take care of things, it will take half the time.

In order to help you with this process, I've summarized all the checklists I use in the Resources section of this book.

The best way to ensure your group's survival is to make the job of organizing and planning it so easy that you never feel a sense of dread or obligation. Plus, when you follow that checklist over and over each week or month, it becomes habit, and habits don't take any energy at all.

An even bigger bonus to recording your processes is succession planning, which we'll talk about in an upcoming section.

Your checklist should include the following elements:

- ☐ The steps you take to plan and broadcast each jam session (see earlier sections on format, using Mailchimp etc.)
- ☐ The steps you take to set up the room, any contacts at your venue, keys etc.
- ☐ The frequency and plan for your concerts
- ☐ The frequency and plan for your community events
- ☐ Group celebrations and traditions you keep, like the Christmas party
- ☐ How often you plan to invite co-leaders to run the group for your succession plan

Join a Community of Other Leaders

As a reader of this book, I'd like to invite you to join our online community of other uke group leaders. Here we will share ideas, inspire each other and help keep up the momentum. Knowing you are not alone in your efforts can be cathartic.

Get instructions to join our online community by going here: http://www.tigardukes.com/leaders

Concerts

Having something to work towards can help you keep up your own momentum and the enthusiasm of your group. In fact, I have several members who LOVE being on stage and have picked TUG because we actively seek concert opportunities. It's one thing to meet every week and play lots of songs. It's another to have a goal to work towards and raise the stakes. I can't think of a better way to keep up the momentum of your group.

Because TUG meets in a Grange hall, we get invited to play concerts for them. This requires no effort on my part. What do you do if your group is not affiliated with a Grange?

Here are some ideas.

Retirement Homes

One of our members' dad lives in a retirement home nearby. I asked her to put me in touch with her contact, Venice. Here's how that call went.

Me: Hi, I'm Joshua and I run a local ukulele group and we're looking for a place to play some music.

Venice: Great. How much do you cost?

Me: Nothing.

Venice: Great! Can you play next Friday?

Retirement homes welcome fun and affordable activities to bring to their residents so getting gigs at retirement homes is easy and has many benefits.

- The audience is VERY forgiving since they are grateful for new entertainment to break their routine. It's a great training ground to try out new songs, or get comfortable on stage.
- The feeling of spreading so much joy is very satisfying. We always have people come up to us after a gig with big smiles telling us how much they've enjoyed our music.
- With luck, you'll be a mature adult someday and may live in a retirement home. Pay it forward!

Marathons

Another idea for finding concert opportunities is with marathons or 5K walks. These events are long, full day affairs whose organizers are struggling to fill the stage with talent. The cool thing about this is that most people in the audience won't even be paying attention to you! They are finishing their race or focused on supporting their runner. Talk about a low-pressure gig.

Other Ideas

The following is a partial list of ideas, I'm sure you can come up with some more on your own:

- Local business conferences
- Farmers markets

- Cafes
- The mall (many retailers hire DJs, why not ukuleles?)
- Flash mob at a local park and get an instant audience of whoever walks by
- Kids parties

Community

Karen Snair, an ukulele player in Montreal, brings up a very great point about how community is the glue that keeps your group together. She says:

> *Creating community is necessary if you want to maintain old members and have new members stay. It's important to create a welcoming friendly atmosphere where members of all levels can feel comfortable. It is for this reason necessary to know the skill level of the members who attend your group. I know of a group where the leader insists on playing 10+ chord songs which results in the club being a place where he is performing to the group because most of his members are beginners and they can't handle the chords he plays. So the first part of community is to make sure all members enjoy playing the songs.*
>
> *Another way to create community is to create apparel that members can wear and show off. For instance t-shirts with the group's logo are wonderful to sell because it enables members to feel as if they are*

part of a group. They come handy when a club attends any ukulele festivals. I've seen clubs sell baseball caps, buttons, hoodies, etc. The possibilities are endless. The rule of thumb is to keep the apparel affordable and attractable. One of the clubs I attend recently was selling t-shirts for about $15, an amount that was very reasonable.

Encouraging conversation before and after the club begins is wonderful because it enables members to get to know each other. It is a good idea to break sometime in the middle of the meeting. This enables people to use the washroom and take a break from playing. Break time is also a great time for members to talk with one another, purchase drinks and other sweets from the venue. If members meet at someone's house, it's a good idea to ask members to donate a couple of dollars to cover the costs the food that is served at break.

One rule of thumb when you announce it is break time, do not pass the microphone to another person to give an announcement unless it relates to the break. If there are other announcements, announce it when the break is over or at the end of the evening before the club breaks for the evening. I know of a case where the leaders announced it was time for a break so a couple of people started talking quietly and then another leader started to make an announcement about additions to the songbook. It had nothing to do with the break and the leader came to them rudely and loudly told the people to be quiet. They were dismissed for break and then they were told to be quiet. It was rudely done and one of the people almost left because of the manner they were treated.

Keeping one's eyes open for ukulele festivals is another way to make connections and meet new people. Even if your club isn't organizing it, showing support by encouraging your members to attend it is a great way to create positive vibes in the community. If the club has some extra money, or time to help organize it, please also help in those ways. I know of one club who doesn't have the greatest reputation because the club's leader refuses to encourage its members to attend the various big festivals in the area.

Another way to create community is to provide telephone lists to the members. One of the local clubs has a telephone list consisting of one's city of residence, telephone number and email address. This enables members to contact each other for lifts and more. They know the list is only for ukulele related subjects and it seems as if people have been respected of it.

Thanks Karen for those awesome ideas.

Community Events

Your group is part of a larger community. There are things happening in your town every day, each one put on by different organizations and often summarized in community newspapers. When community members look at those calendars they are making a decision: to spend time with you playing uke, or to go to swing dancing, or to the street fair, or to the farmers' market, etc.

When you recognize that you are not competing with these other events but complementing them, you can start to plan your events more strategically. For example, if your town has a farmers' market on Sat and Sun from 7 am - 1 pm, then maybe schedule your jam after 1.

Since TUG meets at The Grange, we get invited to play at their annual garden party. We usually have 10 - 15 players on stage; each player invites their family and friends. Attendance at the garden party doubled since they invited us to play. And we only play for 30 minutes. Then we can enjoy the rest of the day getting seeds and tomato starts!

Another time, the local historical society had a summer barbecue and invited us to play for an hour. We got yummy home made food for dinner and shared our music with some of the community's best connected notables.

Think about how your group can fit in between or augment current goings-on in your town.

Celebrate Your Successes

When my book came out, *Job Searching with Social Media for Dummies*, in 2011, I felt a little embarrassed. I'm not sure why. Only that this new role I had as "author" felt foreign to me, or incongruent for me.

That night, our friend and neighbor, Pete, came over with a huge cake and on the cake were little flags with the cover of my book all over it. We cracked open a bottle of whiskey as well, invited some more friends over and it became a party.

I had no intention of celebrating the success I had. But when we did, it felt right. After all, I woke up at 4 am every single day to write for hours before I went to my day job for months and months. I never missed a deadline for my editor. I worked really hard to get the book written well and on time, sacrificing sleep, a social life and time with my family.

When you take the time to build a community, as the leader, this is your own personal success. You are making sacrifices. You might brush it off and say, "Oh, I couldn't have done it without our members." Although this is true, realize that none of them would have done it without you!

Every time we have a potluck or a party I take time to celebrate my success as group leader. When I'm giving the toast before we all eat, I look around the room and make eye contact with each person and feel so incredibly grateful for what they've given me. And then we party! To me, this is a success party, a time to celebrate what I've been able to build with a little vision and a whole lot of perseverance.

I encourage you to feel that pride; the pride in your members for being awesome, and also the pride in your own accomplishment.

After a few months into TUG, I received the following email from one of our members Timark:

Hey-O,

Thank you once again for your generous hosting; this is an awesome little group and it's been fun from the start--such great enthusiasm to move forward into creative spaces. Look at the lives you've affected just by bringing people together; not a small gift my friend.

On we go,

Although this was a small note, it meant the world to me. I don't know if you'll have members like Timark who are generous with their compliments. Know that when your group is up and running, and it's time to pause and look at how far you've come, celebrate that moment.

Mentoring Co-leaders

It's life. Stuff happens. You move, get sick, get bored. Whatever it is, know that nothing lasts forever. And no matter how excited you are about your group right now, at some point you'll need to start thinking about transitioning away from it. It might not be soon, but remember that at some point you will need someone to take over for you.

Look at what happened to the group in the town next to us. The leader got bored and gave the group to one of her members who really didn't have time or willingness to lead. It was a last-minute measure that spelled the end of the group.

For TUG I've put feelers out to see who might take over for me one day. Right now, there's no one in the group willing to commit to it.

I frequently ask members to lead the group when I'm away. When I do this, I'm testing a few things. How quickly the person says, "Yes", how excited they are, and the kinds of feedback I get from the group after they've led. But this isn't all you need to look for. A few years ago, Lily and I went to China for a month of travel. I had to arrange leaders for the four weeks we were away. Not a single person was willing to lead for all four weeks. To me, this means that though they might have been good song leaders, they were not willing to be group leaders.

As Chotel Klobas, founder of STRUM (Seattle's Totally Relaxed Ukulele Musicians) said to me about co-leaders:

> *Burn out is why so many [groups] don't continue. Find what you enjoy doing the most, and let others help what you don't enjoy doing or what you need to get better at. You will find amazing talent everywhere in your group!*

> *I have two wonderful music leaders, they are both strong in something I don't do, one likes Hawaiian, 20's, 30's, and 40's the other 50's-80's.*

> *My co-leaders are Uncle Rod Higuchi (leader, teacher and performer) and Michael Fox (performer and music arranger).*

> *Kimo Hussey gave me some advice when I first started STRUM, which was to keep on developing co-leaders. I didn't think it was needed at first, but now I get it; as life takes people different direc-*

tions Kimo's advice was spot on. So yes, we have several others that are learning to be leaders at any given time. A good leader gives confidence to the other players.

Commitment cannot be trained. And finding someone to fill your shoes when you're gone for good is very hard. In other words, it's not something you wait to figure out. Rather, know that it could take years to find and cultivate this new person.

You can read more about this process here:
http://www.communityclubtoolkit.com/successionplanning.html

Don't Do It Alone

Identify a few of your key members and form a committee to discuss group leadership succession. Don't do it alone. After a few months, you'll know who comes all the time and who has a "yes" attitude. Invite those folks over for tea one day and have a candid conversation about this. Don't expect one of them to step up and commit to taking over. What you're looking for is support in your own choice of a successor. These folks can help you think about a plan to find your next ace.

Your guidance committee will also serve as mentors for the new person after you're gone. They'll look for things like turn over, new members, consistency and tone of communications etc.

Identify the Skills Needed

The first thing to do in your plan is identify the skills required of someone to run your group. Here's an easy template to use:

Importance of position:

Personal Charisma:

Level Commitment (over committed):

Main objective of the position:

Key skills required for this position:

-
-
-

Previous experience that would be beneficial:

Other knowledge required:

_____

Personal qualities or characteristics, which are suitable for the position:

-
-
-

The Succession Plan

You'll want to identify required next steps, a list of possibilities, to-dos and deadlines for your succession plan. Looking ahead at when you may need to hand your group off is a huge part of your checklist and habits. When documenting what you do each week or month, be sure to schedule some time for allowing others to run your group, identifying what skills you can help those people develop and so forth.

Also, and most importantly, all of this documentation can be handed off to your successor. When you ask them to co-lead, hand them your checklist as a way to test that it's complete!

Here's a simple table to help you figure this out:

Successor Name	Current Position	Future Position	Skills/Knowledge to be Developed	Time Frame	Training/Development Required	Deadline for Delivery	Mentor/Person
Josephine McNally (one for each option you identify)	Active group member	Group co-leader	Improve rhythm and counting into songs Song selection to be more inclusive Finger picking to be able to guide orchestrations	1-2 years	James Hill Books 1-3 African drumming How to lead a group workshop at next Uke Festival	Josephine will need to be prepared to take on the new role by the Garden party (20th May). James Hill book 1 completed by January 31	Group Leader Other co-leaders Treasurer and events coordinator

COMMON MISTAKES

Not Changing Your Songs from Time to Time

When we were getting ready for a concert we played a lot of the same songs from week to week. Then even after the concert, I got lazy and kept at it.

Consequently, I got this email:

> *Dear Joshua,*
>
> *Thanks for the leadership of the TUG group; however, it is not quite the group of which I was hoping. A word of explanation might be in order.*
>
> *Most people I believe are into ukuleles for the thrill and fun of it. Your style is to improve and perfect one's style, which is quite honorable. You seem to be saying, "We are going to repeat this song until we get it right!" It's just not what I want to do.*

The routine of repeating over 50% of last week's song for the following week, ad nauseam is not a very interesting way. You really must increase the repertoire and cut WAY back on technical corrections; one or two suggestions per song is about right. FUN, FUN, FUN is the approach to have if you want the group to expand. Even a small coffee/cookie break half way through, would be very nice; conversation and discussion of playing styles or whatever would automatically be started & enhance the meeting.

Thank you for your attention.

Evan

I replied:

Evan,

Thanks for the suggestions. Sorry it didn't work out for you. Perhaps another group would be a better fit.

Good luck,

Joshua

Here's the thing, he's only half right in my opinion. Learning and getting better is FUN. It is fun for me and our members. The point I agree with him on is that I was repeating about 50 percent of the same songs from week to week. That was when I was in my "play the same first and last song" phase. Frankly, I was getting bored, too.

But since he didn't have fun learning or getting better, I really do feel he wasn't a good fit for us. And that's ok.

Based on his email, he wasn't planning to come back and was offering this advice based on a compulsion; perhaps it was to be helpful. I probably would have taken it more seriously if he had said he would come back. It's good to be able to peel away complaining from actual useful suggestions.

I'll admit, I took his email very personally. I was working extremely hard to get the group off the ground and probably could have responded nicer. Lesson learned!

It's a fine balance between pleasing the crowd and doing what you think is right. Often, when you are off course, someone will remind you of it. Be open to the suggestion, correct it only if you agree with it then move on.

Talking About Politics or Religion

I'm not going to go into my views of the most recent presidential election. What I will say is that because I don't EVER talk about politics and religion during jam sessions, no one else does either.

As the leader, I set an unspoken, yet very well understood, precedent that these topics are off limits within the safe space I was creating.

Luckily, we avoided some very upsetting conversations, since as it turned out, we had differing perspectives on the future leadership of this country, right and left both.

Personally, I come to play the ukulele to get away from the seriousness of the world. I have to read all the fake news, personal rants and attacking opinions on my Facebook feed. Let's face it, nobody attending an ukulele jam session wants any of that stuff either. And certainly no one is going to change their mind because of it. At the best, you'll lose members, at the worst, your group dies.

So please, never ever bring up, or allow anyone else to bring up, politics and religion.

A Note About Race

We all know the ukulele came from Hawaii. However, very few of us have participated in uke groups with Hawaiians. Why is that?

Unless you specifically went to a group specializing in Hawaiian music and culture, like the one on Maui called "The 808 Uke Jam" (http://808ukejams.com/classes/) then it's not likely a Pacific Islander will be among us.

I became hyper aware of this when I got an email from an Asian American Leadership group putting on a conference this summer. They took one look at our TUG website and asked me, "Do you have any Pacific

Islanders in your group?" I think their planning committee had made the assumption that an "ukulele group" will be comprised of, well, the people who invented the uke!

I guess they haven't seen videos of many ukulele groups!

Despite the somewhat strange situation I found myself in (1) wanting to play this concert but (2) being the wrong ethnicity, I think there's an important point to learn from this.

The spirit of the ukulele has always been one of Aloha, sharing and welcoming. I'm grateful to the Hawaiian people every time I pick up my instrument because that's a history worth remembering and a value worth living.

Having these thoughts brought me to a conclusion that I can honor the tradition and the gift of the ukulele by playing at least one Hawaiian song per session. The intention is not cultural appropriation, but simply appreciation of the gift from this culture.

I know this isn't much, and certainly I wish I could do more to help first-nation people preserve their rich culture, so I do what I can do. As the leader of an ukulele group, it is my responsibility and my expression of love to bring some of the Hawaiian culture into the lives of others.

Resources

Where to Find Songs

- Halifax Ukulele Songbook is a great place to start: https://halifaxukulelegang.wordpress.com/hug-songbook
- Richard G's Huge Song List: http://www.scorpexuke.com/ukulele-songs.html
- Ukester Brown: http://www.ukesterbrown.com/song-sheets.html
- Doctor Uke gives you the audio and chords: http://www.doctoruke.com/songs.html
- Ukulele Songs: http://www.ukulelesongs.com
- Got A Uke: http://www.gotaukulele.com
- Turlock Uke Jamz: http://www.turlockukejamz.org/songs.html
- Yo!Ukulele: http://yokulele.com/ukulele-song-sheets/
- Ukulele Hunt: http://ukulelehunt.com/blog/
- Chordie: http://www.chordie.com/topsongs.php?cat=Uke+Collections
- Hey Ukulele: http://www.heyukulele.com/free-content/
- Ukutabs: https://ukutabs.com/
- The Ukulele Teacher: https://www.youtube.com/user/TheUkuleleTeacher
- Cynthia Lin: http://www.tigardukes.com/cynthialin

- Got a Uke: http://www.gotaukulele.com
- Jim's Ukulele Songbook: http://ozbcoz.com/Songs/index.php

Checklists and Workflows for Running an Ukulele Group

Here is My Weekly Workflow Using Onsong:

1) On Wednesday, create a new set list and set the date to that of our next jam. This date will become the name of the set list automatically.
2) Add 10-12 songs from my TUG Songbook. I'll talk about how to pick your songs in a later chapter.
3) Export the set list to a Dropbox folder which I've shared with my mailing list called, "This Week's Songs."
4) Get to the jam on Sunday, open up my iPad and all the songs for the week are right there, in the right order, ready to be played.

Adding New Songs to OnSong for our Group Folder

1) Import new songs from a Dropbox folder called, "Put New Songs Here". Sometimes, I'll spend a few minutes formatting the song on my computer to make it more compatible with Onsong.

2) Find ways to convert the song to the Onsong format if possible. This might be importing a new version of the song from Safari, importing a text file or seeing if Onsong can read the document. Worse case scenario, I keep the song in whatever format I found it in.

3) Make sure I note how the song starts and ends either in the Onsong format or as a sticky note.

Weekly Workflow in Mailchimp

5) Duplicate last week's campaign (email), rename it and update the subject line.
6) Write up any important announcements
7) Update the song list from the Onsong set list I just created, see last section
8) Send the email

Anatomy of a Weekly Email to the Group

- Personalized first-name greeting
- Any important announcements like upcoming concerts or community events
- The Dropbox link to the "This Week's Songs" folder
- The song list
- Essential details, like the time and location of the jam, for any new subscribers

Facebook Group Management Checklist

- Approve any new members who've requested to join
- Post something cool and ukulele related, could be a YouTube video, photo of a uke or news
- Comment on someone else's post

The Essential Pages for Your Group's Website

- **Home**, include your newsletter opt-in form
- **Contact us**, your phone number and group's location

- **Song list**, include that Dropbox link to your songs here
- **News** or Blog where you can post photos, videos, articles, guidelines and news. The more content you post, the higher your site will rank on Google.

Steps to Optimize Your Website so Google Can Find You

1) Make sure your website is searchable: head to your Wordpress settings area, click on Reading and make sure search engines can index your site.
2) Take a look at your Divi Theme Settings and update your site's Title, and Subtitle with your keyphrase present.
3) Go to the Edit area for each of the new pages you created. Below the Divi edit area you'll now see the Wordpress SEO settings box. Give each page a different Title and Description which include your location (Tigard) and the words Ukulele or Uke, and club or group.
4) Include a Description for very image you use
5) On the page itself, make sure your written content has keywords, which include your location, "ukulele", and group or club.
6) Post a couple of blog posts. The more content you have the better Google will like you. Posts can be news, such as, "We're starting a new Uke Club in town".
7) Find ways to link to other pages on your site from within other pages. This is called *internal linking*. A fast way to do that is to

refer to the News (blog) section from your home page and have Blog posts refer to the Contact page "for more details."

8) Install a plugin called Divi Custom Footer, and add the name of your group, the address and phone number in your footer. This way, every page will have the most important details.

The TUG Meeting Agenda

1) Introduce new members and go around the circle with names and something to share, maybe something about the uke they are playing today
2) Remind people we need participants for any upcoming performances
3) Remind people to contribute a few bucks to keep the lights on (also at the end)
4) Poll the crowd for the number of walk-in songs we have for the open mic at the end
5) "Let me know if you have other announcements you'd like to make." Sometimes there are up-coming uke related events, lost and found, or news that players want to talk about so open it up for everyone to make announcements
6) After announcements, we launch into our song list for the day
7) Last half-hour is reserved for walk-in songs and open mic

Mental Checklist Before Starting Others in Song

- Hear the song in your head before you start counting, that might mean listening to it the day before to get it stuck in your brain
- Practice with a metronome at home to get better at keeping rhythm
- Note the key and time signature of the upcoming song
- Provide a suggested strum pattern and tempo to the group
- If a song presents an opportunity for an instrumental solo, be sure to ask for volunteers before the song starts
- If not explicitly written on the sheet music, describe the introduction you plan to use to get into the song.
- Note anything unusual about the ending. Often the hardest areas to keep a group playing well together are the start and ending of the tune
- Point out any tricky chords or chord transitions that you noticed in your pre-review at home. Pay attention to facial expressions as you're talking. If people are frowning at their sheet music, ask if they have questions
- Describe any pickup notes and how to count around those, pickup notes are confusing for some people, this is where the song starts before the first beat. Think of Hanalei Moon, "When you" happens before the first beat, "See Hanalei by moonlight". So, you might count this song with "1,2,3,4,1,2 'When you see...'"

- Count into the song loudly and tap your foot if you don't have a drum, and be sure to play the first note and sing the first word, after that, look around the room and make sure everyone is having fun

Directory of All Groups

The following list was compiled from the following four sources and is the first time such a complete list has ever been put into print.

- http://forum.ukuleleunderground.com/forumdisplay.php?21-Regional-Get-Togethers
- http://www.gotaukulele.com/p/ukulele-clubs-and-societies.html
- http://www.ukulelemag.com/club-hub
- http://ukulelehunt.com/2010/03/10/ukulele-clubs-and-groups/

To make a correction, addition or removal from this list please email the author at http://tigardukes.com

---

** Download the PDF version of this entire 50 page directory **
http://www.tigardukes.com/directory

The United States

Alabama, US

Birmingham Ukulele Society	www.facebook.com/groups/488072584630392/
The Tennessee Valley Ukulele Club	www.facebook.com/pages/The-Tennessee-Valley-Ukulele-Club/206465426194965
Ukulele Band of Alabama	www.ubalabama.weebly.com/
Ukulele Library Club	www.facebook.com/Odenville-Ukulele-Library-Club-1746231558978384/

Arizona, US

Jerome Ukulele Orchestra	www.jeromeukuleleorchestra.com
Phoenix Ukulele Meetup Group	www.meetup.com/The-Phoenix-Ukulele-Meetup-Group/
Prescott Ukulele Guild	www.facebook.com/prescottukes/
Sun City Vistoso Ukulele Club	www.suncity-vistoso.com/clubs/ukulele/
Ukulele club	www.scukes.org/

California, US

"Strum!" Ukulele Jam	www.meetup.com/Ukulele-Strum/
Aloha Strummers	www.alohastrummers.wixsite.com/aloha-strummers
Area 525 Ukulele Club	www.facebook.com/Area515UkuleleClub
Baywood Ukulele Social Club (BUSC)	www.baywooduke.blogspot.co.uk/
Berkeley Ukulele Club	www.ukemaker.com/ukeclub/
CCC Ukulele Fellowship	www.meetup.com/cccukulele/
Chico Ukulele Group	www.facebook.com/pages/Chico-Ukulele-Group/194021080644774?sk=timeline
Claremont Ukulele Club	www.claremontukuleleclub.org/

Start Your Ukulele Group

Cowlitz Ukulele	www.facebook.com/CowlitzUkulele
Delta Strummers	www.deltastrummers.org/
E Kanikapila Kākou	www.sites.google.com/site/huihoopaaolelohawaii/hawaiian-phrases
Florida Ukulele Network in Hollywood	www.meetup.com/Florida-Ukulele-Network/
Funstrummers Ukulele Band	www.funstrummers.com/1.html
High Desert Ukes	www.facebook.com/groups/358992695826
Highland Pickers	www.highlandpickers.com
Humboldt Ukulele Group (HUG)	www.anniediver.wixsite.com/humboldtukulelegroup
Kolohe Ukulele Club	www.koloheukuleleclub.org/
Malibu Ukulele Orchestra	www.facebook.com/pages/Malibu-Ukulele-Orchestra/336412733067339
Moonlight Beach Uke Strummers	www.launch.groups.yahoo.com/group/MoonlightBeachUkeStrummers/
Napa Valley Flea Jumpers	www.fleajumpers.wordpress.com/
Ojai Ukulele Orchestra	www.facebook.com/Ojai-Ukulele-Orchestra-1449025122012795/?ref=bookmarks
Sacramento Ukulele's and Stuff	www.meetup.com/Sacramento-Ukuleles-and-Stuff/
San Francisco Ukulele Rebellion	www.meetup.com/San-Francisco-Ukulele-Meetup/
San Jose Ukulele Club	www.sanjoseukeclub.org
SD Ukulele	www.meetup.com/SDUkulele/
SF Peninsula Ukulele Group	www.meetup.com/SF-Peninsula-Ukulele-Group/
Sneaky Tiki Ukulele	www.meetup.com/sneakytiki/
South Bay Strummers	www.meetup.com/SouthBayStrummers
South Shore Ukulelians	www.ukulelesoftahoe.com/
Stringletter Publishing	www.stringletter.com
Temecula Valley Ukulele Strummers	www.temeculaukuleleclub.com
The Coastside Strummers	www.facebook.com/groups/TheCoastsideStrummers/

Directory

The United States

The Delta Strummers	www.deltastrummers.org
The Hau'oli Strummers	www.meetup.com/SDUkulele/
The Jumpin Flea Circus Players Players Of Los Angeles	www.jumpingflea.tumblr.com
The Monterey Ukulele Club	www.montereyukeclub.wordpress.com
The Pluckin' Strummers	www.pluckinstrummers.wordpress.com/
The SLO Strummers of the Ukulele Society of the Central Coast	www.slostrummers.org
The Strum Bums of Grass Valley	www.coolhanduke.com/strumbums.html
The Tri-Valley UKC	www.meetup.com/Tri-Valley-UKC-Ukulele-Club/
Thousand Oaks Happy Little Ukelele Club	www.tohappylittleuke.weebly.com/
Turlock Uke Jamz	www.Turlockukejamz.org
UFO Hana	www.UFOhana.org
Ukulele Club of Santa Cruz	www.UkuleleClub.com
Ukulele Friends Ohana (UFO)	www.meetup.com/Ukulele-music-group/
Ukulele Jam LA	www.meetup.com/Ukulele-Jam-LA/
Ukulele Society of America (USA)	www.launch.groups.yahoo.com/group/Ukulele_Society_of_America/
Ukulele University	www.ukeuniversity.com
Ukulele University / River City Ukes	www.meetup.com/UKEUniversity/
Ukuleles Of Paradise	www.ukuleletonya.com/blog/ukuleles-of-paradise
Ukuleles of Tahoe	www.ukulelesoftahoe.com/
Valley Ukulele Society	www.facebook.com/groups/ValleyUkuleleSociety
West Country Ukulele Club	www.facebook.com/groups/223727658128

Colorado, US

Arvada CO Ukulele Song Circle	www.groups.yahoo.com/neo/groups/Arvada_CO_Ukulele_Song_Circle/info
Colorado River Uke Group	www.meetup.com/Colorado-River-Uke-

Start Your Ukulele Group

	Group/
Denver Uke Community	www.launch.groups.yahoo.com/group/UkuleleCommunityDenver/
Fort Uke	www.meetup.com/FortUKE
Rocky Mountain Ukulele Orchestra	www.ukuleleorchestra.org
The Denver Uke Community	www.Den-Uke.com
Ukulele Orchestra	www.ukuleleorchestra.org/orchestra/

Connecticut, US

Bristol Ukulele Club	www.orgsites.com/ct/bristol-ukes/
Glastonbury Ukulele Club	www.doctoruke.com/gluc.html
Motor City Ukes	www.motorcityukes.com/

Florida, US

Boggy Creek Swampers Ukulele (Saint Cloud)	www.facebook.com/groups/141384869651996/
Boynton Delray Uke Society	www.facebook.com/groups/BoyntonUkeSociety/
East Pasco/Hernando Ukulele Club	www.meetup.com/East-Pasco-Hernando-Ukulele-Club/
Fernandina Ukulele Network (FUN)	www.facebook.com/Fernandina-Ukulele-Network-FUN-910699122333676/?ref=ts&fref=ts
Florida Ukulele Network Citrus Tower	www.meetup.com/Florida_Ukulele_Network_Citrus_Tower/
Florida Ukulele Network Hollywood	www.meetup.com/Florida-Ukulele-Network/
Florida Ukulele Network in Palm Beach	www.meetup.com/fun4ukulele/
Florida Ukulele Network in SpaceCoast	www.meetup.com/Ukulele-SpaceCoast/
Florida Ukulele Network Miami	www.meetup.com/Florida-Ukulele-Network-in-Miami/

The United States

Pensacola Ukulele Players Society (PUPS)	www.gulfweb.net/rlwalker/PensacolaUkulelePlayersSociety/index.html
Spacecoast Ukulele Club	www.meetup.com/Space-Coast-Ukulele-Club/
Sun coast Sand Fleas	www.facebook.com/groups/suncoastsandfleas/
Tampa Bay Ukulele Society (TBUS)	www.meetup.com/tampabayukes/
Ukes St Andrews	www.facebook.com/ukes.standrews1?fref=ts
Ukulele Club of Gainesville	www.facebook.com/ukuleleclubgville
Ukulele Luau of Jacksonville	www.meetup.com/Jacksonville-Ukulele-Luau/

Georgia, US

Golden Isles Strummers	www.facebook.com/gistrummers/
South East Ukers	www.southeastukers.weebly.com

Hawaii, US

Ukulele Club of Kona	www.launch.groups.yahoo.com/group/meleohana/
Boise Ukulele Group	www.boiseukulelegroup.com
Mele Ohana	www.groups.yahoo.com/neo/groups/meleohana/info

Idaho, US

Boise Ukulele Group	www.boiseukulelegroup.com

Illinois, US

Chicago Ukulele Cabaret	www.ukechicago.org/
Chicago Ukulele Group	www.facebook.com/groups/199488831131

Start Your Ukulele Group

(CHUG)	
Free Range Ukulele Society Of Oak Park	www.freerangeukulelesociety.com
Normal Uke Jam	www.normalukejam.com/
North Shore Ukes	www.facebook.com/ChicagoNorthShoreUkuleleSociety?ref=br_tf
Oak Park Ukulele Meetup Group	www.meetup.com/Oak-Park-Ukulele-Meetup-Group/
Quad City Ukulele Club	www.facebook.com/QCUkeClub
Rock River Strummers	www.ukulelestationamerica.com
Springfield Uketopians	www.meetup.com/Springfield-Uketopians/events/145418412/
Tuesday Ukulele	www.facebook.com/TuesUkulele/
UJM Ukulele Club	www.meetup.com/ujmukeclub/
Ukulele Players In Decatur	www.facebook.com/groups/372974653078478/

Indiana, US

Batesville Memorial Public Library Ukulele Club	www.ebatesville.com
Bloomington Ukulele Club	www.sites.google.com/site/ukuleleclubloomington
Indianapolis Ukulele Fans (The Indy Ukers)	www.facebook.com/groups/386057376528

Iowa, US

Muscatine Area Ukulele Group	www.facebook.com/Muscatine-Area-Ukulele-Group-220742148268860/?ref=hl

Kansas, US

Kansas City Ukesters	www.kcuke.com

The United States

Pittsburg Ukulele Club	www.facebook.com/pages/Pittsburg-Ukulele-Club/578267745593941
Ukulele Fight Club of Kansas City	www.facebook.com/groups/225354030843745/
Wichita Ukulele Society	www.facebook.com/groups/wichitaukulelesociety

Kentucky, US

Cool Hand Ukes	www.meetup.com/NKY-Unplugged-Acoustic-Society/events/154491282/
Lexingtones Uke Group	www.facebook.com/groups/Lexingtones
Lousiville Ukulele Club	www.facebook.com/groups/259925724048458/

Louisiana, US

The Houma / Thibodaux Ukulele Association	www.facebook.com/groups/1791253841201286/
Ukulele Gumbo	www.ukulelegumbo.com

Maine, US

Bucksport Ukulele Club	www.facebook.com/pages/Bucksport-Ukulele-Club/1543851022550251?sk=timeline
Oxford Hills Ukulele Group	www.sites.google.com/site/oxfordhillsukulelegroup/
The FLUKES (Falmouth Library Ukulele Ensemble)	www.facebook.com/thefalmouthflukes
Ukes Midcoast Maine	www.facebook.com/ukes.midcoastmaine
Ukulele Club of Brunswick	www.ukesofbrunswick.weebly.com/index.html

Maryland, US

Alexandria Ukulele Club	www.facebook.com/AlexandriaUkuleleClub/
Baltimore Ukulele Club	www.facebook.com/groups/903957823027692/
Brunswick Ukulele Jam	www.facebook.com/Brunswick-Ukulele-Jam-1617014745211396/?fref=ts
Chestertown Ukulele Club	www.facebook.com/Chestertown-Ukulele-Club-668348286588293/
Easton Ukulele Club	www.facebook.com/pages/Easton-Ukulele-Club/1412618125687326
HCPL Ukulele Club	www.hcplonline.evanced.info/signup/eventdetails?eventid=20925&lib=0&return=
Maryland Ukulele Jam	www.mdukejam.shutterfly.com/
NoVA Uke	www.NoVA-Uke.org
UkeAnnapolis	www.ukeannapolis.wordpress.com

Massachusetts, US

Featherstone Ukulele Jam	www.facebook.com/groups/657301394353507/

Michigan, US

Ann Arbor / Ypsilanti Ukulele Group	www.ukulele.meetup.com/85/
Glug Head	www.facebook.com/groups/glughead/
Grukes	www.facebook.com/groups/grukes/
Happy Ukulele Group Grand Rapids	www.facebook.com/groups/grukes/?hc_location=ufi
Lake-O Ukers!	www.facebook.com/groups/486051228118511/
LAUGH - Lansing Area Ukulele Group	www.benhassenger.com/laugh/
Mid Michigan Ukulele Group Strum	www.facebook.com/groups/mmugs/

The United States

SUGAR - Saginaw Ukulele Gurus And Rookies	www.facebook.com/SUGARSaginawUkuleleGurusAndRookies/
The Ann Arbor Ypsilanti Ukulele Group	www.ukulele.meetup.com/85/
The Lansing Area Ukulele Group (L.A.U.G.H.)	www.facebook.com/group.php?gid=256534770353
Ukulele 85	www.meetup.com/ukulele-85

Minnesota, US

StrumMn Ukulele Players	www.strummn.shutterfly.com
Twin Cities Ukulele Club	www.bluegrassfun.com/twin-cities-uke-club.html
Two Harbors Ukulele Group	www.twoharborsukulelegroup.com/
Twin Cities Ukulele Club	www.tcukeclub.com

Missouri, US

Battle Creek Ukulele Group Bugs	www.groups.yahoo.com/group/BUGS/join
Drury University's Ukulele Club (DUke	www.facebook.com/DruryDUkes
Holland Ukulele Group Strum	www.facebook.com/groups/HollandUkulele/
Kansas City Ukesters	www.kcuke.com
Queen City Ukulele Club	www.springfield-music.com/new-at-springfield-music/queen-city-uke-club/
St. Louis Ukulele Group	www.facebook.com/groups/250602162075
The Kansas City Ukesters in Missouri	www.kcuke.com
Ukulele Fight Club of Columbia	www.facebook.com/groups/532266126856667/
Ukulele Fight Club of Greater St. Louis	www.facebook.com/groups/124147887620237/
Ukulele Fight Club of Jefferson City	www.facebook.com/groups/604541576331148/

Lansing Area Ukulele Group (L.A.U.G.H.)	www.facebook.com/groups/256534770353

Montana, US
Butte Ukulele Club	www.buttepubliclibrary.info/

Nebraska, US
Lincoln Ukulele Group	www.groups.yahoo.com/neo/groups/Lincoln_Ukulele_Group/info
Omaha Ukulele Club	www.meetup.com/OmahaUkes/

Nevada, US
Ninth Isle Ukulele Club	www.meetup.com/Ninth-Isle-Ukulele-Club/
The Ukulele Club of Las Vegas	www.meetup.com/ukulele-club-of-las-vegas

New Jersey, US
Morristown Uke Jam	www.facebook.com/MorristownUkeJam/
South Jersey Ukulele Circle	www.facebook.com/SouthJerseyUkuleleCircle
Ukulele Club of Westfield & Central N.J.	www.meetup.com/Ukulele-Club-of-Westfield-and-Central-New-Jersey/

New Mexico, US
Las Cruces Ukes	www.lascrucesukes.blogspot.co.uk
Santa Fe Ukulele and Social Club	www.facebook.com/SantaFeUkuleleandSocialClub/

The United States

New York, US

Buffalo Ukulele Club	www.meetup.com/buffaloukuleleclub/
Cal-Mum Ukulele Club	www.gstboces.org/toolbox/template.cfm?ID=2990
Catskills Ukulele Group	www.meetup.com/Catskills-Ukulele/
Crunch Banana Uke Group	www.cnyuke.com
Ithaca Ukes	www.facebook.com/IthacaUkes/
Long Island Ukulele Strummers Club	www.sites.google.com/site/islandukeclub
New York City Ukulele Meetup Group	www.meetup.com/NYCUkuleleJam/
Salt City Ukulele	www.saltcityukulele.org
Spa City Ukulele Brigade	www.facebook.com/SpaCityUkes
SUNY Plattsburgh Uke-A-Dooks	www.facebook.com/sunyplattsburghukeadooks
The All Boro Ukuleles (TABU)	www.meetup.com/ukulele-81/
Buffalo Ukulele Group	www.facebook.com/groups/452251478174255/

North Carolina, US

Buckeye Ukulele Society	www.meetup.com/BuckeyeUkuleleSociety/
Carolina Ukulele Ensemble	www.uncstudentorgs.collegiatelink.net/organization/ukulele/about
Cleveland Ukulele Group	www.clevelandjumpingflea.blogspot.co.uk
Durham Ukulele Group	www.durhamukulelegroup.blogspot.com/
Greater Charlotte Ukulele Meetup	www.charlotteuke.com
North Carolina Ukulele Academy	www.AlohaU.com/
The Dancing Fleas Ukulele Club	www.facebook.com/dancingfleas

Ohio, US

Buckeye Ukulele Society	www.meetup.com/buckeyeukulelesociety

Start Your Ukulele Group

Cleveland Jumping Flea	www.clevelandjumpingflea.com/
Cool Hand Ukes of NKY	www.meetup.com/NKY-Unplugged-Acoustic-Society/
NEOUKES	www.meetup.com/Lorain-County-Ukulele-Group

Oklahoma, US

OKC Ukulele Club	www.facebook.com/groups/OKCUke
Stillwater Ukulele Association	www.facebook.com/StillwaterUkuleleAssociation?fref=ts
Tulsa Ukulele Club	www.tulsaukes.blogspot.co.uk/

Oregon, US

Bend Ukulele Group	www.facebook.com/BendUkuleleGroup/info
Cowlitz Ukulele	www.facebook.com/CowlitzUkulele
North Eugene Ukulele Orchestra	www.facebook.com/NEHSUkes
Portland Ukulele Association	www.home.teleport.com/~pua/
Salem Ukulele Strummers Association (SUSA)	www.salemukes.com/
Tigard Ukulele Group	www.tigardukes.com
Ukulaneys - Ukulele Club of Lane County	www.brookadams.com/static_ukulaneys.html
Ukulele Fans of Oregon	www.ukulelefansoforegon.com

Pennsylvania, US

Allegheny Ukulele Kollective	www.alleghenyukes.com/
Central PA Ukulele Club	www.facebook.com/groups/241326099319143/
Greater Philly and Central NJ Ukulele Ensemble	www.facebook.com/groups/154442274609890/
Mainline Ukulele Group	www.meetup.com/mainlineukulelegroup
Mid-Jersey Ukulele Circle	www.facebook.com/Mid-Jersey-Circle

The United States

Morristown Uke Jam	www.meetup.com/MorristownUkeJam/events/187125512/
N.W.P.A Ukuleles	www.nwpaukuleles.com
Philadelphia Fishtown Ukulele Club	www.meetup.com/Fishtown-Ukulele-Club-Philadelphia/
Philadelphia Main Line Ukulele Group	www.meetup.com/mainlineukulelegroup
Steel City Ukuleles	www.meetup.com/Steel-City-Ukuleles/
The Central Pennsylvania Ukulele Club	www.facebook.com/#!/groups/241326099319143/
Tri-state Ukeclectics Uke Club	www.facebook.com/groups/1897776930443652/
Ukulele Jam	www.clayonmain.org/event-calendar/ukelele-jam-half-moon-cafe-5/
Ukulele Uprising	www.sites.google.com/site/ukeuplanc/

South Carolina, US

The Greater Charlotte Ukulele Meetup Group	www.meetup.com/charlotteuke/

South Dakota, US

Kazukes	www.facebook.com/pages/Kazukes/231362806951574

Tennessee, US

Chatta Ukes	www.facebook.com/ChattaUkes/timeline
Memphis Ukulele Flash Mob	www.facebook.com/groups/609872215793573/?hc_location=ufi
Nashville Ukulele Society	www.nashukes.blogspot.co.uk

Texas, US

Austin Ukulele Society	www.austinukulelesociety.wordpress.com

Start Your Ukulele Group

Dallas Ukulele Headquarters	www.meetup.com/ukulele-84/
Galveston Ukulele	www.galvestonukulele.com
Hearts Home Acoustics	www.HeartsHomeAcoustics.com
Highland Lakes Ukulele Club	www.sites.google.com/site/highlandlakesukuleleclub/
Houkulele	www.houkulele.com
Padre Island Duke Club	www.padreislandukeclub.com
San Antonio Ukulele Meetup Group	www.meetup.com/San-Antonio-Ukulele-Meetup-Group/
The Dallas Ukulele Headquarters	www.ukulele.meetup.com/84/

Utah, US

UFO HUM	www.ufohum.ukuleleplay.com/
Utah County Uke Club	www.facebook.com/groups/uc.uke.club/?hc_location=ufi
Utah Ukulele Association	www.utahukuleles.com

Virginia, US

Alexandria Ukulele Club	www.facebook.com/AlexandriaUkuleleClub/?ref=aymt_homepage_panel
Charlottesville UVA Ukulele Lodge	www.meetup.com/Charlottesville-UVA-Ukulele-Lodge/members/62032662/
G.R.O.U.P (Greenbrier River Optimistic Ukulele Players)	www.ukuleleoptimists.com
Midnight Ukulele Society	www.midnightukulelesociety.yolasite.com
North Virginia Ukulele Society	www.meetup.com/NoVA-Uke-Ensemble/
Peninsula Ukulele Players	www.facebook.com/groups/VApups/permalink/1308435279180681/
River City Ukulele Society	www.facebook.com/groups/rivercityuke/
Star City Ukulele Circle	www.facebook.com/groups/starcityukecircle

The United States

Washington, US

Bellingham Ukulele Group	www.bellinghamukulelegroup.com/
Fidalgo Ukulele Network	www.fidalgoukulelenetwork.com
Monday Ukulele Ohana	www.facebook.com/mondayukuleleohana
Olympia Aloha Ukulele Players	www.facebook.com/OlyAUP
Salmonberry Band	www.salmonberryband.weebly.com/
Seattle Ukulele Players Association (SUPA)	www.seattleukulele.org/index.html
Seattle's Totally Relaxed Ukulele Musicians (STRUM)	www.facebook.com/STRUMthatuke/
UkeVerse	www.facebook.com/groups/1996869290540516/
Ukolympians	www.facebook.com/Ukolympians
Ukulele Players of The Palouse	www.facebook.com/UkulelePlayersOfThePalouse
Ukulele Sing-A-Long Circus	www.singingbarista.wix.com/ukecircustacoma
Ukuleles Unite!	www.ukulelesunite.com
WASSUP (Washington Association of South Sound Ukulele Players)	www.launch.groups.yahoo.com/group/WASSUP-Ukers/

Wisconsin, US

Cheez Land Uke Band	www.cheezlandukeband.com
Fans Of U.K.E - The Ukulele Klub of Eau Claire	www.facebook.com/pages/Fans-of-UKE-The-Ukulele-Klub-of-Eau-Claire/193993083963603?fref=ts
Lake Country Ukulele Club	www.facebook.com/groups/cooneyukesters/
Madison Area Ukulele Initiative (MAUI)	www.MAUImadison.com/index.html
Mid Michigan Ukulele Group Strum (MMUGS)	www.facebook.com/groups/mmugs/
Milwaukee Ukulele Club	www.facebook.com/group.php?gid=70868967721
Oconomowoc Ukulele Club	www.facebook.com/groups/cooneyukest

The Ukulele Klub of Eau Claire (U.K.E.)	ers/ www.ukewis.com/
Ukulele Society of Door County	www.ukulelesocietyofdoorcounty.com

Wyoming, US

Happy Ukulele Group of Grand Rapids	www.facebook.com/groups/grukes/

The United Kingdom

Aberdeen City, UK
Aberdeen Ukes	www.facebook.com/groups/aberdeenukes/

Alresford, UK
Alresford Ukulele Jam	www.facebook.com/alresfordukejam

Bedford, UK
Ukulele Bedford	www.ukulelebedford.co.uk/

Bedfordshire, UK
Aroha2Aloha	www.aroha2aloha.co.uk/home.html
Sandy Ukulele Group (S.U.G)	www.SandyUkuleleGroup.com
Ukes of Buzzard	www.facebook.com/pages/The-Ukes-of-Buzzard/1543054272637165
Ukie-Toones	www.ukietoones.org.uk
Ukulele Bedford	www.ukulelebedford.co.uk

The United Kingdom

Berkshire, UK

Kingsclere Ukulele Group	www.kingsclere.ukuleles.org.uk/
Newbury Ukuleles	www.newbury.ukuleles.org.uk/
Reading Ukulele Group	www.readingukulelegroup.co.uk/
The Small Strings	www.facebook.com/TheSmallStrings
Uke's of Windsor	www.facebook.com/windsorukulelegroup/
Woodley Ukulele	www.woodleyukulele.wordpress.com/

Billingham, UK

Aroha2Aloha	www.facebook.com/Aroha2aloha

Birmingham, UK

Moselele	www.moselele.co.uk/

Blackpool, UK

Blackpool George Formby Branch	www.blackpoolgeorgeformbybranch.com/

Bolton, UK

Bolton Ukulele Group	www.facebook.com/groups/boltonukulelegroup/

Bournemouth, UK

Bournemouth Ukulele Social	www.susbus.co.uk

Bradford, UK

The Bradford Ukes	www.facebook.com/#!/groups/the.bradfor

Directory

Start Your Ukulele Group

d.ukes

Braintree, UK

Uke on the Brain	www.ukeonthebrain.org.uk/

Bridgend, UK

Maesteg Ukulele Club	www.maestegukulele.club/

Bridgnorth, UK

Bridgnorth Strummers & Ukulele Band	www.ukuleleband.co.uk

Brighton, UK

BAD ukes	www.bad-ukes.moonfruit.com/#/home/4546677299

Bristol, UK

Bristol Ukulele Jam	www.facebook.com/pages/Bristol-Ukulele-Band/816567611773433

Buckingham, UK

Buckingham Ukulele Group (The Old BUGers)	www.facebook.com/groups/1426184174355106/

Buckinghamshire, UK

Aylesbury Uke Jam	www.sites.google.com/site/aylesburyukejam/
Buckingham Ukulele Group (The Old BUGers)	www.facebook.com/BuckinghamUkuleleGroup2014?fref=pb&hc_location=profile_browser

The United Kingdom

Haddenham Ukulele Musos	www.sites.google.com/site/haddenhamukulelemusos/
Marlow Ukulele Group	www.marlowuke.co.uk/
MK Lele	www.groupspaces.com/mklele/
Three Counties Ukulele Players (TCUPS)	www.facebook.com/groups/tcupsgb/

Cambridge, UK

Cambridge Ukulele	www.facebook.com/CambridgeUkulele

Cambridgeshire, UK

The Misspent Ukes	www.facebook.com/TheMisspentUkes
The Palmerston Ukulele Band	www.palmyukeband.com

Cardiff, UK

Ukulele Nights	www.ukenights.co.uk
Ukulele Wolves Cardiff	www.facebook.com/groups/1816071071943372/

Chelmsford, UK

Ukulele Pub Jam Session	www.davidwarren202.demon.co.uk/ukulele.htm

Cheltenham, UK

UkeGlos – Gloucestershire's Ukulele Club	www.cheltuke.co.uk/

Cheshire, UK

Ageless Ukes	www.facebook.com/groups/570263326393618/?fref=ts

Directory

Start Your Ukulele Group

Burton Ukulele Band	www.facebook.com/BurtonUkuleleBand?fref=pb&hc_location=profile_browser
Congleton Uke Players	www.facebook.com/groups/517560771788531/?ref=bookmarks
Macclesfield Ukulele Club	www.maccuke.co.uk/
Neston Ukes	www.facebook.com/nestonukes
U3A Beartown Ukes	www.congletonu3a.org.uk/
Holmes Chapel Ukulele Group	www.facebook.com/HCUkuleles/

Chessington, UK

The Guitar and Uke Group	www.guitarandukesession.wordpress.com

Chester, UK

Strictly Ukes	www.strictlyukes.com/

County Durham, UK

Durham City Uke Group	www.facebook.com/durhamcityukegroup/
Harlepool Ukulele Group	www.facebook.com/pages/Hartlepool-Ukulele-Group-HUG/160656254084005?ref=br_rs
Stockton to Darlington Ukulele Express	www.ukuleleexpress.blogspot.com/

Cumbria, UK

Bryce Street Strummers (Burnside)	www.burneside74.wix.com/strummers
Carlisle Ukulele Club	www.carlisleukeclub.webs.com
Cockermouth Ukuleles	www.cukes.co.uk/
South Lakes Ukulele Orchestra	www.facebook.com/southlakesukuleleorchestra
The Bryce Street Strummers	www.burneside74.wix.com/strummers
Ukes Akimbo	www.facebook.com/ukesakimbo

The United Kingdom

Ukes Of Allonby	www.facebook.com/groups/ukesofallonby/

Darlington, UK

Stockton to Darlington Ukulele Express	www.ukuleleexpress.blogspot.com/

Derby, UK

Derby Ukulele Club	www.derbyukuleleclub.weebly.com/index.html

Derbyshire, UK

Beehive Ukulele Club	www.facebook.com/groups/RipleyandbelperUkes
Glossop Ukulele Group (GLUG)	www.glossopug.wordpress.com/

Devon, UK

Babbacombe Ukulele Strummers	www.babbacombeukulele.co.uk/
Budleigh Ukulele Strummers Club	www.busc.weebly.com/
Dawlish Ukulele Folk	www.dawlishukulelefolk.wordpress.com/
Exeter Ukulele Club	www.exeterukuleleclub.com/
Hatherleigh Ukulele Bashers	www.hatherleighukulelebashers.net
Ilfracombe Ukulele Club	www.facebook.com/pages/Ilfracombe-Ukulele-Club/243448482369768
Plymouth Ukulele Players	www.plymouthuke.yolasite.com
Ukulele Orchestra Of South Dartmoor	www.facebook.com/ukuleleorchestraofsouthdartmoor

Start Your Ukulele Group

Dorset, UK

Bournemouth Ukulele Social (SUSBUS)	www.susbus.co.uk/
Bridport Ukulele Group	www.bridportukulelegroup.org.uk/
Corfe Hills Ukulele Group	www.m.facebook.com/Corfehillsukulelegroup?ref=bookmarks
Dorset Ukulele Jam	www.dorsetukulelejam.co.uk
Lyme Regis Ukulele Group	www.lymeluggersukulele.co.uk/
Poole Ukulele Pluckers & Strummers (PUPS)	www.pooleukes.wixsite.com/pups
Shaftesbury Ukulele Band	www.theukeshack.co.uk/
The Luggers	www.lymeluggersukulele.co.uk
Weymouth Ukuleleans	www.facebook.com/groups/WEYMOUTHUKULELEANS
Wimborne Ukulele Band	www.theukeshack.co.uk/
Witchampton Ukulele Orchestra	www.facebook.com/groups/513272252034239/

East Riding Of Yorkshire

Hull Ukulele Group (HUG)	www.hullukulelegroup.wordpress.com/
Ukulele Junction	www.facebook.com/WeAreUkuleleJunction

East Sussex, UK

Cool Hand Ukes	www.coolhandukes.co.uk/
Rye Ukulele Experiment	www.ryeukuleleexperiment.co.uk
Ukulele Kollective Eastbourne	www.facebook.com/ukulelekollectiveeastbourne
Wadhurst Ukulele Group	www.wadhurstukulelegroup.wordpress.com

Edinburgh, UK

Monday Ukearist	www.ukearist.wordpress.com/

Enfield, UK

S.O.U.P.	www.ukulelesoup.co.uk

Essex, UK

Clacton Ukulele Club	www.facebook.com/ClactonUkes
Colchester Ukulele Academy	www.colchester-ukulele-academy.co.uk
Dovercourt Ukulele Club	www.facebook.com/pages/Dovercourt-ukulele-club/169008006586188?hc_location=ufi
Maldon Ukulele Group (MUGs)	www.facebook.com/maldonukulelegroup?_rdr
Uke On The Brain	www.ukeonthebrain.org.uk

Glasgow, UK

Glasgow Ukulele Society	www.facebook.com/group.php?gid=120785867936274&v
Scottish Multicoloured Ukulele Troop (SMUT)	www.facebook.com/pages/Scottish-Multicoloured-Ukulele-Troop-SMUT/242711280525?ref=ts

Gloucestershire, UK

At Cross Keys Inn	www.facebook.com/crosskeysinngloucester
Cheltenham Ukulele	www.cheltuke.co.uk
The Ukes uv 'Azzard	www.facebook.com/groups/1595607733989686/
Uke.Stroud	www.ukestroud.wordpress.com
Ukulele Jam Thornbury	www.ukulelejam.co.uk

Godalming, UK

You Ukes	www.you-ukes.org.uk/home.html

Start Your Ukulele Group

Greater London, UK

Hammersmith Ukulele Group	www.hammeruke.github.io/
Hanwell Ukulele Group	www.hanwellukulele.co.uk/
London Branch of George Formby Society	www.georgeformby.co.uk/

Greater Manchester, UK

Bolton Ukulele Group	www.boltonukulelegroup.tumblr.com
Levenshulme Uke Up	www.levenshulmeukeup.tumblr.com/
Phoenix Ukulele Club	www.phoenixukes.weebly.com
Stockport Ukulele	www.stockportukulele.btck.co.uk/
Stretford	www.facebook.com/StretfordUkeGroup/timeline
Uke Too	www.oldham.gov.uk/learning/music-service/ukelele.htm
Wigan Ukulele Club	www.wiganukuleleclub.co.uk/

Hampshire, UK

Alresford Ukulele Jam	www.facebook.com/AlresfordUkeJam?fref=photo
Hayling Huggers Ukulele Group	www.haylinghuggers.com/
Hythe Ukulele Group	www.hytheukulelegroup.org.uk/about-hug/
Kingsclere Ukulele Group	www.kingsclere.ukuleles.org.uk/
Lymington Ukulele Hangout	www.ukulelehangout.webs.com
Milford Strummers	www.milfordstrummers.co.uk/
Milton Ukulele Strummers Klub (MUSK)	www.peteflunky.wix.com/musk
Portsmouth Ukulele Jam	www.portsmouthukulele.co.uk
Southampton Ukulele Jam	www.suj.btck.co.uk/
Stokes Bay Strummers	www.facebook.com/TheStokesBayStrummers/
Streetlife Ukulele Group Songsters (SLUGS)	www.facebook.com/groups/1626739297547405/

The United Kingdom

Ukulele Hangout	www.ukulelehangout.webs.com
Waterside Ukulele Jam (Hythe)	www.watersideukulelejam.co.uk/
Winchester Uke Jam	www.moonroller.com/winchesterukejam.htm

Hertfordshire, UK

Berkhamsted Ukulele Random Players (BURP)	www.burpmusic.com/
Bishops Stortford Ukulele Society	www.bsus.co.uk/
Herts Of Uke	www.sites.google.com/site/hertsofuke/home
The Ukulele Society of Great Britain	www.usgb.co.uk/
Ver Players	www.verplayers.org.uk
Ware Ukulele Group	www.wareukegroup.co.uk

Isle Of Wight, UK

Wight Ukers	www.facebook.com/groups/isleloveukes/

Jersey, UK

Jersey Ukulele Club	www.facebook.com/groups/JerseyUkuleleClub.2014/

Kent, UK

Abbey Ukulele Players	www.janetipayne.wix.com/abbeyukeplayers
Bay City Ukers	www.baycityukers.blogspot.co.uk/
Benenden and Iden Green Ukulele Jam	www.facebook.com/groups/BIGUKE/
Crock ham Hill Ukulele Musical Society Chums	www.royaloakcrockhamhill.co.uk/?p=162
Headcorn Ukulele Group (HUG)	www.headcornukulelegroup.com
Invicta Ukulele Club	www.invictaukuleleclub.co.uk

Start Your Ukulele Group

Kent Ukulele and Banjulele Appreciation Society (KUBAS)	www.kubas.co.uk/
Man of Kent Ukuleles	www.facebook.com/groups/MOK.UKES/
Market Inn Strummers	www.facebook.com/pages/Market-Inn-Strummers/834924526534954
Marmite Ukulele Club	www.marmiteukuleleclub.com
SaltDish Ukulele Group	www.facebook.com/pages/SaltDish-Ukulele-Group/325129604338284?ref=br_rs
Sevenukes	www.sevenukes.com/
St Hilda's Ukulele Group	www.sthildasukes.com
Thanet Ukulele Club	www.facebook.com/ThanetUkuleleClub?ref=br_rs
Tunbridge Wells Ukulele Night Thing (TWUNT)	www.facebook.com/groups/twunt/
Ukelear SUBs	www.facebook.com/Ukelear-SUBs-1520455954905111/?__mref=message_bubble
Darent Valley Youth Music Ukulele Orchestra	www.dvym.org/the-bands/1917-2/

Kidderminster, UK

Severnside Ukulele Strummers Association	www.spanglefish.com/kidderminsterukuleleclub/

Kingston upon Hull, UK

Barely Awake Ukulele Group	www.u3asites.org.uk/awake/page/48925
Hull Ukulele Group (HUG)	www.hullukulelegroup.wordpress.com

The United Kingdom

Knoydart, Highlands, UK

The Knoydart Ukuleles	www.facebook.com/pages/The-Knoydart-Ukuleles/245950382126031

Lancashire, UK

Blackpool George Formby Branch	www.blackpoolgeorgeformbybranch.com/
Clitheroe Ukulele Club and Orchestra	www.clitheroeukuleleclub.com
Fleetwood Ukulele Network (FUN)	www.facebook.com/groups/ukulelefun/
Morecambe Ukulele Club	www.facebook.com/groups/morecambeukuleleclub/
Ormskirk Ukulele Club	www.ormskirkukuleleclub.org.uk
Preston Ukulele Strummers Society (PUSS)	www.facebook.com/events/313912304362/
The B.U.G Club (Banjo, Ukulele, Guitar)	www.facebook.com/groups/bugclub/?__mref=message_bubble
Ukes At The Wharf	www.facebook.com/pages/Ukes-At-The-Wharf/837746122967752?fref=ts
Woodplumpton Ukulele Players	www.facebook.com/groups/929325223785465/

Warwickshire, UK

Spa Strummers Ukulele Group of Leamington Spa	www.spa-strummers.co.uk/index.html

Leicester, UK

South Leicester Ukulele Group & Singers (S.L.U.G.S.)	www.slugs.club/

Leicestershire, UK

Flukes Ukulele Collective	www.facebook.com/groups/410411995679514
Great Central Strummers	www.loughboroughukes.weebly.com/
MHUG	www.mhug.co.uk
Oakham Ukulele Club	www.oakhamukuleleclub.weebly.com
The First Monday Ukulele Club	www.facebook.com/pages/The-NUkes-First-Monday-Ukulele-Club/198688520189670

Lewisham, UK

People of Lewisham's Ukulele Club (PLUC)	www.lewishamukulele.wordpress.com/

Lincolnshire, UK

Horncastle Ukulele Group	www.facebook.com/groups/267187783490111/?ref=bookmarks
Lincoln Ukulele Band	www.lincolnukuleleband.co.uk/
Lincoln Ukulele Club	www.facebook.com/lincolnukuclub?ref=br_rs
Sleaford Ukulele Orchestra	www.myspace.com/sleafordukuleleorchestra
Ukulele Orchestra of Spalding	www.facebook.com/pages/Ukulele-Orchestra-Of-Spalding/112436028808939

Liverpool, UK

NW Charity Singers Uke Club	www.nwcsukeclub.co.uk/
Ukulele Club Liverpool	www.facebook.com/ukuleleclubliverpool

London, UK

Balham - Balham Ukulele Society	www.facebook.com/groups/balhamukesoc

The United Kingdom

Bar Kick Uke Jam	www.myspace.com/barkickukejam
Bexley Ukulele Group (BUG)	www.facebook.com/bexley.ukulelegroup
Brockley Ukulele Group	www.brockleyukegroup.blogspot.com/
Charing Cross Road - Ukulele Wednesdays	www.ukulelewednesdays.com
Croydon Ukulele Jam	www.ukulele.magix.net/
Dulwich Ukulele Club	www.facebook.com/thedulwichukuleleclub
Enfield - S.O.U.P	www.users.waitrose.com/~radavenport/soup/
Great Portland Street - Ukulele Wednesdays	www.ukulelewednesdays.com
Grosvenor Ave - Ukey Love	www.ukeylove.com/
Hanwell Ukulele Group	www.facebook.com/groups/420557001375658/
Kendall Green - Kensall Rise Ukulele Massive	www.facebook.com/thekrumclub?ref=br_rs
Kings Cross - Ukulele Kings Cross	www.facebook.com/UkuleleKX?ref=br_rs
Lewisham - People Of Lewishams Ukulele Collective	www.lewishamukulele.wordpress.com/
North London Ukulele Collective	www.facebook.com/groups/172367906204668/
Bar Kick Uke Jam	www.myspace.com/barkickukejam
Teddington Ukulele Players (TUP)	www.facebook.com/groups/TeddingtonUke/
Karauke	www.karauke.co.uk
Ukulele Wednesdays	www.ukulelewednesdays.com

Mansfield, UK

Mansfield Ukulele Group (MUGs)	www.mansfieldukulelegroup.co.uk/

Merseyside, UK

Grateful Fred's Ukelear Deterrent	www.facebook.com/GratefulFredsUkelearDeterrent

Directory

Start Your Ukulele Group

Greasby Ukes	www.facebook.com/Greasby-Ukes-338217909669317/?ref=tn_tnmn
Ma Egertons Uke Jam	www.facebook.com/dukesofhazzardukulele
MADUkes	www.facebook.com/MADUkesmaghull/?ref=ts&fref=ts
NW Charity Singers Uke Club	www.nwcsukeclub.co.uk
St Helens Ukulele Group	www.st-helens-ukulele-group.co.uk
Ukulele Club Liverpool	www.ukuleleclub.org.uk
Wirral Ukulele Club	www.wirralukuleleclub.com
Wirral Ukulele Fanatics	www.facebook.com/WirralUkuleleFanatics

Middlesbrough, UK

Middlesbrough Happy Ukulele Group	www.facebook.com/groups/585197241586717/

Milton Keynes, UK

MK Lele	www.groupspaces.com/mklele/

New Milton, UK

MUSK Milton Ukulele Strummers Klub	www.peteflunky.wix.com/musk

Newcastle, UK

Occupy Ukulele at the Rosetti Studio (OURS)	www.facebook.com/groups/OccupyUkulele/
Sunday Ukes (Newcastle upon Tyne)	www.ukes4fun.org.uk/

Newton, UK

Newton Abbot Ukulele Club	www.ukulelesocialclub.ning.com/profile/steveNewtonAbbotUkuleleClub

Directory

The United Kingdom

Norfolk, UK

Fenland Ukuleles (FLUKES)	www.fenlandukuleles.co.uk
Flukes	www.flukes.org.uk/
Harleston U3A Ukuleles	www.u3asites.org.uk/code/u3asite.php?site=106&page=33956
Kings Lynn Ukulele Club	www.facebook.com/groups/KingsLynnUkuleleClub/
Norwich Ukulele Society	www.facebook.com/groups/224409327130/
The Seaside Strummers Ukulele Group	www.facebook.com/The-Seaside-Strummers-Ukulele-group-1156507927722970/info/?tab=page_info
The Ukulele Monthly	www.facebook.com/theukulelemonthly/

North Yorkshire, UK

Cleveland Ukulele Fraternity	www.clevelandukulele.co.uk/
Grand Old Uke Of York	www.gouyclub.wordpress.com
Harrogate Spa Town Ukes	www.facebook.com/Harrogate-Spa-Town-Ukes-289500407873226/
Middlesbrough Happy Ukulele Group	www.facebook.com/groups/585197241586717/
Minster Ukes	www.facebook.com/minsterukes/
Redcar Ukes	www.redcarukes.wordpress.com
Scarborough Ukulele Club (Seaside Uke Strummers)	www.seasideukestrummers.weebly.com
Skipton Ukulele Club	www.facebook.com/SkiptonUkuleleClub
University Of York Ukulele Group	www.facebook.com/pages/University-of-York-Ukulele-Group/1492869510997675?ref=br_rs
York Orchestra Of Ukulele	www.york-orchestra-of-ukulele.co.uk/Links/

Northampton, UK

Northampton Ukulele Group NUGs	www.thenugs.co.uk/

Northamptonshire, UK

Daventry Ukulele Society (Dukesukes)	www.dukesukes.co.uk
NHS Ukulele Club	www.facebook.com/NHSjammers/timeline
Northampton Ukulele Group NUGs	www.thenugs.co.uk
Raunds Ukulele Orchestra	www.sites.google.com/site/raundsukulele/home

Northern Ireland, UK

Omagh Ukulele Orchestra	www.facebook.com/Omagh-Ukulele-Orchestra-551355958399786/
Uke Belfast	www.facebook.com/belfastukes?fref=ts
Ukulele Strings - meet at Playhouse Theatre	www.derryplayhouse.co.uk

Northumberland, UK

Bay Uke	www.facebook.com/groups/1537555709835701/
Core Music	www.coremusic.co.uk/
Hexham Uketeers	www.facebook.com/The-Hexham-Uketeers-1861346200754241/?ref=page_internal
The Old Ship	www.theoldshipnewbigginbythesea.org.uk/#/ukelele-night/4549901678
The Uke Of Northumberland	www.ukeofnorthumberland.wordpress.com
Wooler Ukulele Angel Delights	www.facebook.com/TheSchoolOfUke

Nottage, UK

Porthcawl Ukulele Band	www.facebook.com/pages/Porthcawl-Ukulele-Band/279132437655?ref=search&sid=548493639.1980450277..1

Nottingham, UK

Nottingham Ukulele Club	www.nottinghamukeclub.com/

Nottinghamshire, UK

Mansfield Ukulele Group (MUGs)	www.facebook.com/groups/376776749183099/
Newukes	www.facebook.com/NewUkesUK
Nottingham Ukulele Club	www.nottinghamukeclub.com/
Retford Ukulele Group	www.facebook.com/groups/RetfordUke/
U3A Newark Ukulele	www.u3anewarkukulele.co.uk/

Oxford, UK

Oxford Ukuleles	www.oxfordukuleles.co.uk/

Oxfordshire, UK

Hooky Ukes	www.hook-norton.org.uk/ai1ec_event/hooky-ukes/?instance_id=
International Ukulele Club of Sonning Common	www.facebook.com/pages/Sam-Browns-International-Ukulele-Club-of-Sonning-Common/176352412387298
Oxford Ukuleles	www.oxfordukuleles.co.uk/
The Peoples Ukulele Brigade	www.facebook.com/groups/305650789482962/

Poole, UK

Dorset Ukulele Jam	www.dorsetukulelejam.co.uk/

Start Your Ukulele Group

Poole Ukulele Pluckers & Strummers (PUPS)	www.pooleukes.wix.com/pups

Preston, UK
Woodplumpton Ukulele Players	www.facebook.com/groups/929325223785465/

Reading, UK
Reading Ukulele Group	www.readingukulelegroup.co.uk/

Redcar and Cleveland, UK
Cleveland Ukes	www.clevelandukulele.weebly.com/

Ringwood, UK
Ringwood Ukulele Hangout	www.ukulelehangout.webs.com

Scotland, UK
Ayrshire Ukulele Clan	www.facebook.com/pages/Ayrshire-Ukulele-Clan/1652123641668947?hc_location=ufi
Crieff Ukulele Group	www.facebook.com/crieffukulelegroup
Earlston Ukulele Club	www.facebook.com/Earlston-Ukulele-Club-EUC-608491015988915/
Edinburgh Uni Ukulele Group	www.facebook.com/EdinburghUkes
Fife Ukulele Orchestra	www.facebook.com/pages/Fife-Ukulele-Orchestra/326285044144448
MML Ukulele Club	www.moraymusiclessons.com/mml-ukulele-club/
Monday Ukearist	www.ukearist.wordpress.com/about/
Peebles Uke Group	www.sites.google.com/site/peeblesuke/

The United Kingdom

West Of Scotland Ukulele Players (WOSUP)	www.facebook.com/groups/WOSUP

Sheffield, UK

Sheffield Ukulele Sundays	www.ukulelesundays.co.uk/

Shropshire, UK

Community Uke (Pontesbury)	www.communityuke.org.uk
Cool and Uke (Coalbrookdale)	www.facebook.com/coolandukeclub
High and Mighty Uke Club	www.anitafoster66.wix.com/high-and-mighty-uke
Shropshire Ukulele Massive	www.facebook.com/ShropshireUkuleleMassive/
The Belle V'Ukes	www.facebook.com/thebellevukes?hc_location=ufi
The Brickaleles	www.brickaleles.weebly.com
The Cool and Uke Club	www.facebook.com/coolandukeclub

Somerset, UK

Bath Ukulele	www.facebook.com/groups/252348808153939/
Burnham on Sea Seaside Strummers	www.facebook.com/UkulelesinBurnhamonsea
Carpe Uke	www.facebook.com/Ukulele-group-Carpe-Uke-424015787790821/?fref=ts
Frome Ukulele Club	www.facebook.com/Fromeukuleleclub
Taunton Ukulele Strummers Club (TUSC)	www.tusc.co.uk/
Yeovil Ukulele Club	www.facebook.com/groups/1556439904592158/?fref=ts

South Shields, UK

North East Branch of the George Formby Society	www.facebook.com/pages/North-East-George-Formby-Society/233835399966377

South Wales, UK

Lions Club Caerphilly	www.e-clubhouse.org/sites/caerphilly/

South Yorkshire, UK

George Formby Society - Sheffield Branch	www.facebook.com/groups/GFSSheffieldBranch/
Ukulele Sundays	www.ukulelesundays.co.uk/

Southampton, UK

Southampton Ukulele Jam	www.southamptonukulelejam.co.uk
Hythe Ukulele Hangout	www.ukulelehangout.webs.com

Southsea, UK

Pompey Pluckers	www.pompeypluckers.org
Portsmouth Ukulele Jam	www.portsmouthukulele.co.uk/

Spalding, UK

Ukulele Orchestra of Spalding	www.ukuleleorchestraofspalding.co.uk/

Staffordshire, UK

Biddulph Ukulele Group	www.b-u-g.org.uk/
Burton on Trent Ukulele Group	www.bukegrupe.blogspot.co.uk/
Zoticus in Leek	www.facebook.com/Zoticus-in-leek-1608445629458344/

The United Kingdom

Stockport, UK
Stockport Ukulele	www.stockportukulele.btck.co.uk/

Suffolk, UK
Ipswich Ukulele Collective	www.facebook.com/ipswichukulelecollective
Somerleyton Ukulele Strummers	www.facebook.com/SomerleytonUkuleleStrummers
The Ukes of Southwold	www.facebook.com/groups/1669346160061484/

Surrey, UK
UkeJam	www.facebook.com/ukejam#!/ukejam
You Ukes	www.you-ukes.org.uk/home.html

Swindon, UK
Old Town Ukes	www.oldtownukes.co.uk/
Swindon Ukulele Club	www.ukeboxjury.co.uk/ubjwebsite/swindonukeclub.htm

Taunton, UK
Taunton Ukulele Strummers Club (TUSC)	www.tusc.co.uk/

Teddington, UK
Teddington Ukulele Players (TUP)	www.facebook.com/groups/TeddingtonUke/

Telford and Wrekin, UK

High and Mighty Uke Club	www.anitafoster66.wix.com/high-and-mighty-uke

Thornbury, UK

Ukulele Jam Thornbury	www.ukulelejam.co.uk/

Tyne and Wear, UK

Bay Uke	www.facebook.com/groups/1537555709835701/
Newcastle City Library Ukulele Class	www.facebook.com/groups/304528166558743/
Occupy Ukulele at the Rosetti Studio (OURS)	www.facebook.com/groups/OccupyUkulele/
Tune Army Ukulele Club	www.tunearmy.blogspot.com/
Ukes4Fun (Byker)	www.ukes4fun.org.uk/

Wakefield, UK

Wakefest	www.facebook.com/Wakefest-1646024755662586/timeline/

Wales, UK

Absolute Beginners Ukulele Group	www.facebook.com/Absolute-Beginners-Ukulele-Group-785025228297862/
Bangor Ukulele Society	www.facebook.com/groups/Bangorukulelesociety
Blaneau Gwent Rhythm and Ukes	www.facebook.com/groups/1418744085087131/
Blukulele	www.ukeplanet.co.uk/category/blukulele/
Bridgend Ukulele Club	www.facebook.com/bridgendukes
Cherry Pickers Ukulele Band	www.facebook.com/CherryPickersUkuleleBand/

The United Kingdom

Colwyn Bay Ukulele Group	www.facebook.com/pages/Colwyn-Bay-Ukulele-Group/153001054714857?ref=br_rs
Haverford West Ukulele Club	www.facebook.com/Haverfordukeclub?ref=br_rs
Maesteg Ukulele Club	www.maestegukulele.club
Neath Ukulele Club	www.facebook.com/neathukuleleclub?ref=br_rs
Pembrokeshire Ukulele Pirates (Pups)	www.facebook.com/pages/Pembrokeshire-Ukulele-Pirates/508173255891247
Porthcawl Ukulele Band	www.porthcawlukuleleband.com
Swansea Ukulele Group	www.facebook.com/groups/SwanseaUkuleleClub
The Buskuleles of Usk	www.facebook.com/buskuleles
Ukulele Nights	www.ukenights.org.uk

Walsall, UK

Sandwelele Ukulele	www.facebook.com/groups/732885046847424/

Warwickshire, UK

Earls Of Uke	www.facebook.com/EarlsOfUke
Harbury Ukulele Club	www.harburyukulele.me.uk
Spa Strummers Ukulele Group of Leamington Spa	www.spa-strummers.co.uk

West Berkshire, UK

Uke's of Windsor	www.facebook.com/windsorukulelegroup

West Midlands, UK

Black Country Ukulele Group	www.halesowenuke.yolasite.com/
Blackheath Ukulele Collective	www.bukec.weebly.com/

Start Your Ukulele Group

Blackheath Ukulele Group	www.bug-strummers.webnode.com/
Halesowen Ukulele Group Strummers (HUGS)	www.halesowenuke.yolasite.com/
Penn Ukulele Club	www.pennukeclub.webs.com/index.htm
Sedgley Ukulele Strummers	www.sedgley-strummers.co.uk
The Black Country Ukulele Players	www.facebook.com/pages/Black-Country-Ukulele-Players/179909585402963?sk=wall

West Sussex, UK

Chichester Ukulele Group	www.chichesterukeclub.co.uk/
East Grinstead Ukukele Club	www.facebook.com/groups/EGukeclub/
Hukuberry Jam	www.hukuberry.co.uk
Littlehampton Ukulele Jam	www.facebook.com/groups/110408865675226/
Uke at the Duke	www.ukeattheduke.co.uk
Weald Ukulele Players and Singers	www.wups.info/
Wukulele - Worthing's Ukulele Jam	www.wukulele.com

West Yorkshire, UK

Baildon Ukulele Club	www.baildon-ukulele-club.com/
Groove @ The Grove	www.ukulele-grove.com
Haworth Ukulele Group (HUG)	www.facebook.com/groups/haworthukulelegroup/
Meanwood Ukulele Club	www.yourukuleletutor.com/spartcart/product/meanwood-ukulele-club-8-x-15-hour-sessions.htm
Moortown Ukulele Club	www.yourukuleletutor.com/spartcart/product/thursday-night-ukulele-club-8-x-2-hour-sessions.htm
Otley Ukulele Orchestra	www.otleyukuleleorchestra.wordpress.com
Roundhay Ukulele Club	www.roundhayukulelegroup.wordpress.com
Shelley Village Over 60's	www.shelleyukuleleband.wordpress.com

Directory

The United Kingdom

Ukulele Club	
The Bradford Ukes	www.facebook.com/TheBradfordUkes
The Chemic Ukulele Group (CHUG)	www.facebook.com/groups/TheCHUG/
The Merrie Pluckers	www.facebook.com/themerriepluckers/?hc_location=ufi
Wake UP	www.facebook.com/groups/147766532077274/

Whickham, UK

Tune Army Ukulele Club	www.tunearmy.blogspot.com/

Whyteleafe, UK

Surrey Ukulele Banjo Society	www.freewebs.com/surreyukulelebanjosociety/

Wigan, UK

Phoenix Ukulele Club	www.phoenixukes.weebly.com/

Wiltshire, UK

Ashton Keynes Ukulele Strummers	www.ashtonkeynesukulelestrummers.co.uk
Chippenham Ukuleles	www.sites.google.com/site/cukuleles/
Melksham Ukulele Social Club (MUSC)	www.musc.info
Old Town Ukes	www.oldtownukes.co.uk/index.htm
Salisbury Ukulele Band	www.theukeshack.co.uk/
Swindon Ukulele Club	www.ukeboxjury.co.uk/ubjwebsite/swindonukeclub.htm

Start Your Ukulele Group

Winchester, UK

Winchester Uke Jam	www.winchesterukejam.co.uk

Windham County, UK

The Dancing Flea Orchestra, West Cornwall	www.facebook.com/dancingfleaorchestra

Wirra, UK

Wirral Ukulele Fanatics	www.facebook.com/WirralUkuleleFanatics

Worcestershire, UK

Harvington Ukulele Group	www.facebook.com/HarvingtonUkuleleClub/info?tab=page_info
Worcester Ukulele Club	www.worcester-uke-club.co.uk

Worthing, UK

Wukulele - Worthing's Ukulele Jam	www.wukulele.com/

York, UK

Grand Old Uke of York	www.grandoldukeofyork.info

Yorkshire, UK

Harrogate Spa Town Ukes	www.facebook.com/pages/Harrogate-Spa-Town-Ukes/289500407873226

Australia

Australian Capital Territory, AUS

Gay and Lesbian Ukulele Band (GLUB)	www.meetup.com/GLUB-Gay-and-Lesbian-Ukulele-Band-Canberra/
Ukulele's Canberra	www.meetup.com/UkulelesCanberra/
TUGS Ukulele	www.tugsukulele.com

New South Wales, AUS

Albury Wodonga Uke Muster	www.alburywodongaukemuster.com
North Coast Ukulele Collective	www.ukulelecollective.com
Goulburn Ukulele Group	www.ronmclaughlin.wix.com/grubukuleles
Lismore Ukulele Club	www.facebook.com/LismoreUkuleleClub?sk=info
Uke Mullum	www.ukemullum.com/
Murrumbidgee Ukulele Group Strummers	www.facebook.com/MUGSGriffith?ref=br_rs
Albury Wodonga Uke Muster	www.alburywodongaukemuster.com/index.html
Balmain Ukulele Klub (BUK)	www.balmainukuleleclub.com.au/
Hawke's Bay Ukulele Underground	www.facebook.com/hbukuleleunderground?fref=ts
Hungry Head Ukesters	www.facebook.com/hungryheadukeband/?fref=ts
Illawarra Ukulele Club	www.ukuleleillawarra.org
Kariong Learn to Play Uke4Fun	www.uke4funinfo.wixsites.com/home
LakeMacUkestra	www.thesumoftheparts.com.au/
Northside Ukulele Team Sydney (NUTS)	www.facebook.com/northsideukuleles
Port Macquarie Ukestra	www.portmacukes.wordpress.com
Silver Ukulele Strummers	www.silverukulelestrummers.com/

Start Your Ukulele Group

St George and Sutherland Community of Ukulele Musicians (SSCUM)	www.meetup.com/SSCUM-ukulele-club/events/46673042/
Sydney Ukulele 'n' beer meetup	www.facebook.com/groups/143179111373/
The Blue Mountains Ukulele Club	www.bluemuc.ning.com/
The Grafton Ukettes	www.facebook.com/The-Grafton-Ukettes-Ukulele-Group-633791313299452/
The Hornsby BUGS	www.hornsbybugs.com/
Uke Central	www.ukecentral.info
Uke Mullum	www.ukemullum.com/
Ukulele's Canberra	www.meetup.com/UkulelesCanberra/
Wollongong Ukulele Group	www.swingaleles.ning.com/
Central Coast Ukulele Club	www.centralcoastukuleleclub.wordpress.com/
Sussex Ukulele Players	www.facebook.com/groups/1030204800360860/
Petersham Ukulele Group	www.facebook.com/groups/162726047071990/
Troubalukers	www.troubadour.org.au/?page_id=22

Northern Territory, AUS

Darwin Ukulele Kollective (DUKes)	www.facebook.com/groups/darwindukes/10153696713877756/
The Dukes - Darwin Ukulele Kollective	www.facebook.com/groups/darwindukes

Queensland, AUS

Brisbane Ukulele Musicians Society (BUMS)	www.brisbaneukulele.com/
Bulimba Ukulele Group	www.facebook.com/pages/Bulimba-Ukulele-Group-BUG/286213164741049
Sunnybank Ukulele Players	www.sunnybankukuleleplayers.wordpress.c

Bulimba Ukulele Group	om www.facebook.com/pages/Bulimba-Ukulele-Group-BUG/286213164741049?ref=br_rs
Cairns Holloways Ukulele Group (CHUG)	www.facebook.com/Cairns-Holloways-Ukulele-Group-at-Strait-on-the-Beach-1410158555964025/timeline/
Coolangatta	www.tableofknowledge.org/Table_of_Knowledge/Ukulele_Club.html
Hill Folk Club	www.wafolk.iinet.net.au/clubs.html
Ukulele Perth	www.ukuleleperth.com/
Cairns Ukulele Club	www.myspace.com/cairnsukuleleclub
Coolangatta Ukulele Players	www.coolangattaukuleleplayers.blogspot.co.uk/
Gold Coast Ukulele Players (G-CUP)	www.gcup.hinternet.com.au/
Gold Coast Ukulelians	www.meetup.com/ukulelians/
Maleny Ukulele	www.facebook.com/MalenyUkulele
Maleny Ukulele Pioneers	www.facebook.com/UkulelePioneersMaleny
Redland City Ukuleles (RCU's)	www.facebook.com/RedlandsCityUkuleleGroup/timeline
Sunnybank Ukulele Players	www.sunnybankukuleleplayers.wordpress.com/playing-nights-events/
Sunshine Coast Ukulele Masters	www.scum.org.au
Townsville Ukulele Club	www.townsvilleukuleleclub.org.au/
Ukulele Pioneers	www.facebook.com/UkulelePioneersMaleny/?ref=aymt_homepage_panel
Beenleigh Ukulele Group	www.facebook.com/Beenleigh-Ukelele-Group-1895465414010269/
Toowoomba Ukulele Group	www.facebook.com/UkuleleGroupe
Ukulele Townsville	www.facebook.com/group.php?gid=295781776478

South Australia, AUS

Adelaide Ukulele Appreciation Society	www.auas.wordpress.com
Bubble & Squeak	www.facebook.com/RiverlandUkulele
The Kukes - The Kensi Ukes	www.facebook.com/groups/316277911857408/
Ukulele Club Of Goolwa (UGG)	www.goolwaukuleles.wordpress.com
Blue Lake Ukulele Ensemble	www.facebook.com/groups/1501435793516665/
Penola Ukulele Club	www.penolaukulelegroup.webs.com
Adelaide Ukulele Appreciation Society	www.auas.wordpress.com
Port Augusta Music Club	www.facebook.com/PortAugustaMusicClub
The Northern Ukuleles (NUkes)	www.thenorthernukuleles.blogspot.com.au

Tasmania, AUS

CHUM (Channel & Huon Ukulele Mob)	www.au.groups.yahoo.com/group/h-u-g/
Hobart Ukulele Group (HUG)	www.hug2007.wordpress.com

Victoria, AUS

Ballarat Ukulele Group	www.ballaratukulelegroup.org
Bendigo Uke Group	www.bendigoukegroup.com
Uke Joint Jumpers	www.ukejointjumpers.com
Bayside Ukes	www.baysideukes.com
Albury Wodonga Uke Muster	www.alburywodongaukemuster.com
Ballarat Ukulele Group	www.ballaratukulelegroup.org/
Bayside Ukes	www.baysideukes.com/
J-Ukes	www.girgarre.com.au
Kalulu Uke Lovers	www.facebook.com/Kalulu.Uke.Lovers/
Melbourne Ukulele Kollective	www.muk.com.au/index.html
Uke 'n Sing	www.welcometomusic.net
Ukes n more	www.ukesnmore.com

Warrnambool Ukulele Group (WUG)	www.warrnamboolukulelegroup.wordpress.com/
Yarra YUkers	www.greatbigukes.com/yarra-yukers/

Canada

Alberta, CAN

Edmonton Ukulele Circle	www.edmontonuke.wordpress.com

British Columbia, CAN

Nanaimo Ukulele Circle	www.ukecircle.com
Coquitlam Ukulele Tiny Instrument Enthusiasts	www.cutiecircle.com/
Vancouver Ukulele Circle	www.vcn.bc.ca/vanukes/index.html
The Cutie Circle	www.cutiecircle.com
Heritage Uke Club	www.ukejoints.blogspot.ca
Vancouver Ukulele Circle	www.vcn.bc.ca/vanukes/index.html
White Rock Ukulele Circle	www.facebook.com/White-Rock-Ukulele-Circle-288931871131723/
Beachcombers Ukulele Group Sunshine Coast (BUGs)	www.facebook.com/BUGs
Glug head	www.facebook.com/groups/glughead/
The Penticton Ukulele Group	www.facebook.com/pentictonukulele
Uke Joints	www.ukejoints.blogspot.ca/

Manitoba, CAN

Ukulele Club of Winnipeg	www.facebook.com/groups/4933619484/?fref=ts

Newfoundland and Labrador, CAN

St John's Ukulele Club	www.facebook.com/groups/276089395042/

Nova Scotia, CAN

Halifax Ukulele Gang (H.U.G.)	www.halifaxukulelegang.wordpress.com/
Saturday Morning Ukulele Group (SMUG)	www.smugpei.blogspot.co.uk/

Ontario, CAN

Kingston Ukulele Society	www.kingstonukes.com/
Lanark Ukulele Group	www.lanarkukulelegroup.com
Corktown Ukulele Jam	www.torontoukes.wixsite.com/torontoukes
Dundas - String Along Ukulele	www.stringalongukulele.ca
Kingston Ukulele Society	www.kingstonukes.com/
London - Ukes of London	www.ukesoflondon.ca/wp/
Northumberland Ukulele Orchestra (NUkeO)	www.facebook.com/groups/75709855409/
Orilla - S.Unshine U.kulele N.etwork	www.sunshineukuleles.wordpress.com
Perth Country Ukulele Group	www.facebook.com/PerthUke
Renfrew Ukulele Group	www.renfrewukegroup.ca/
Sunshine Ukulele Network	www.sunshineukuleles.wordpress.com/
Southern Ontario Ukulele Players	www.londonsoup.weebly.com/
Uke Waterloo	www.sites.google.com/site/ukewaterloo/home
Bytown Ukulele Club	www.bytownukulele.ca/
Petawawa Ukulele Circle	www.petawawaukulele.wordpress.com
Peterborough Ukulele Club	www.facebook.com/groups/119670711486304/

Canada

Dover Uke Heads	www.doverukeheads.com/
Scarborough Uke Jam	www.scarboroughukes.com
Toronto North Ukulele Jam	www.torontoukes.com
Askennonia Senior Centre Ukulele Band	www.askennonia.com
Bugstrum	www.sites.google.com/site/bugstrum/home
Poacher Ukulele Band	www.facebook.com/poacherukuleleband
Renfrew Ukulele Group	www.renfrewukegroup.ca/
Saskatoon Ukulele Friends	www.saskatoonukuleleclub.com
Southern Ontario Ukulele Players	www.londonsoup.weebly.com/
The Ukulele Consortium of Napanee	www.facebook.com/groups/253403544813293/

Quebec, CAN

After Dinner Ukulele Society	www.adukes.org
South Shore Ukulele Club	www.facebook.com/ukuleleclubrivesud
Ukulélé Club de Montréal	www.ukuleleclubdemontreal.com/
Ukulele Club De Quebec	www.facebook.com/Ukuleleclubdequebec
Ukulélé Club Rive-Sud	www.facebook.com/ukuleleclubrivesud/?fref=ts
Ukulele Club de Quebec	www.ukuleleclubdequebec.weebly.com

Saskatchewan, CAN

Queen City Ukes	www.qcukes.com

Yukon, CAN

Uke On Ukulele Club	www.ukeonukuleleclub.weebly.com/

Other Regions Around the World

Argentina

Ukulele es Alegría	www.facebook.com/groups/ukelele esalegria/

Belgium

Brukulele	www.brukulele.be
Ukulele Sur Meuse	www.ukulelesurmeuse.wordpress.com

Finland

Finnish Ukulele Network – FUN	www.ukulele.fi/
Karkkilan I Ukuleleorkesteri	www.facebook.com/Karkkilan-I-Ukuleleorkesteri-463841007151001/
Ukulele Express	www.trevapplingen.nsu.fi/ukulele_express/

France

Club Olympique de Ukulele de Lille et des environs (COULE)	www.coule.fr/
Club Ukulele de Lyon	www.lukedunum.wordpress.com
Uke'n'Play	www.ukenplay.tumblr.com
Les Fondus du Ukulele Nantais	www.les-fondus-du-ukulele-de-nantes.over-blog.com
Nuke Ukulele Explosion	www.nuke06.wordpress.com
Rendev'UKE a Paris	www.rendevuke.wordpress.com
Ukulélé Social Club de Picardie	www.ukulpic.fr/
Véritable Orchestre d'Ukulélé de Saint Denis d'Anjou	www.ukeasaintdenisdanjou.org
Agneaux a son Ukulélé Club	www.lesrendezvoussoniques.com/le-club-ukulele-d-agneaux-aux-rendez-vous-soniques.html

Other Regions Around the World

Association Ukuleles Valbonne Sophia Antipolis (Alpes Maritimes)	www.vsalele.org/
Les Caféléles de Strasbourg	www.mydoghasflea.net/sitecafelele
TOP5	www.top5.re/
Ukulele Fun Box of Bordeaux	www.ukulelebordeaux.com
Ukulele Hui	www.ukulele.fr/
Ukulele in 47	www.myspace.com/ukuleleen47
Ukulele Social Club Oleron	www.mydoghasflea.net/wiki/index.php5?title=Clubs_Associations_Rencontres_Ukulele
Véritable Orchestre d'Ukulélé de Saint Denis d'Anjou	www.ukeasaintdenisdanjou.org/

Germany

Deutcher Ukulelenclu	www.ukulelenclub.de

Hong Kong

Hong Kong Ukulele Socials Meetup	www.meetup.com/Hong-Kong-Ukulele-Socials-Meetup/

Ireland

Arklow - The Arklow Ukulele Players	www.facebook.com/TheArklowUkulelePlayers/
Arklow Ukulele Players	www.ronan.ie
Dun Laoghaire, Co. Dublin - Ukuhooley	www.ukeireland.com/eden-park-stags-head-meetups/
The Hotspot Ukes	www.facebook.com/thehotspotukes
Uke Ireland	www.ukeireland.com/
Ukuhooley	www.facebook.com/UkuHooley

Italy

Ukulele Club Vicenza	www.ukuleleclubvicenza.blogspot.c

Start Your Ukulele Group

om/

Japan

Kyoto Singing Around the Table and New Ukulele Club	www.facebook.com/kyotoukulele/

Malaysia

Johorean Ukulele	www.facebook.com/groups/johoreanukulele/
Labuan Beaufort Ukulele Group	www.facebook.com/groups/189247297833775/
Perak Ukulele Group	www.facebook.com/groups/perakUkelele/
Sabah Ukulele Group	www.facebook.com/groups/orkesakiuku/
Malaysia Ukulele Group	www.malaysiaukulelegroup.com/p/about-mug.html

Netherlands

Amsterdam Ukulele Players	www.aup.jouwweb.nl
Groningen Ukulele Society	www.groningenukulelesociety.com
Amsterdam Ukulele Café	www.facebook.com/ukulelecafeamsterdam
Amsterdam Ukulele Club	www.ukuleleclub.org
Amsterdam Ukulele Players	www.aup.jouwweb.nl/
Delft Ukulele Club (My Clog Has Fleas)	www.mycloghasfleas.nl/
Groningen Ukulele Society	www.groningenukulelesocietyblog.wordpress.com/
Haagse Ukuleleclub	www.ukuleleclub.nl
Official Ukulele Orchestra Dordrecht	www.facebook.com/UkuleleOrchestraDordrechtOud
Parkstad Ukulele Club	www.gady.nl/puc/

Norway

Vestfold Ukuleleklubb	www.ukuleleklubben.com

New Zealand

Uke N Sing	www.singforjoy.org.nz/uke.php
Gisborne Ukulele Underground	www.facebook.com/Gisborne-Ukulele-Underground-607416402694238/
Katitkati Ukulele Group	www.facebook.com/KatikatiUkuleleGroup/?fref=ts
Manwatu Ukulele Group	www.mugsite.org.nz
Morrinsville Ukulele Group	www.facebook.com/Morrinsville-Ukulele-Group-1531733487155594/
Ukubays	www.facebook.com/groups/399555800102008/?fref=ts
Ukulele Heaven - Shorecooleleles	www.facebook.com/ukuleleunion/timeline
Ukulele Sundays	www.facebook.com/pages/Ukulele-Sundays/353449294670992
Rotorua UkeBox	www.facebook.com/rotoruaukebox/?fref=ts
Thermaleles	www.facebook.com/Thermaleles
Ukes On Fire	www.facebook.com/UkesOnFire/
Wanaka Ukuleles	www.facebook.com/Wanakaukuleles/
Hutt Valley Ukulele	www.facebook.com/uke4us/
The Ukulele Institute	www.facebook.com/theukuleleinstitute
Wellington Ukulele Club	www.facebook.com/wellington.ukulele.club
Wellington Ukulele Peace Network	www.meetup.com/Wellington-Ukulele-Peace-Network-NZ/

Start Your Ukulele Group

Eleluku	www.facebook.com/Eleluku-141723849280324/?fref=ts
Dargaville Ukulele Group	www.dargavilleukulelegroup.org.nz
Dunedin Ukulele Club	www.dunedinukuleleclub.blogspot.com
Eleluku	www.facebook.com/pages/Eleluku/141723849280324
Hawkes Bay Ukulele Underground	www.facebook.com/hbukuleleunderground
Katitkati Ukulele Group	www.facebook.com/KatikatiUkuleleGroup/
Manawatu Ukulele Group (MUG!)	www.pncc.govt.nz/news-events-and-culture/communitydirectory/manawatu-ukulele-group-mug/
Plinkers Ukulele Group	www.facebook.com/pages/Plinkers/107939789266215?sk=info
St Kilda Ukulele Lovers League	www.facebook.com/StKildaUkuleleLoversLeague/
Ukes of Howick	www.facebook.com/pages/Ukes-Of-Howick/218204914873186?sk=wall&filter=1
Ukubays	www.facebook.com/groups/399555800102008/
Ukulele Geraldine	www.ukulelegeraldine.co.nz/
Wellington Ukulele Collective	www.facebook.com/wellington.ukulele.club/

Philippines

Ukulele Philippines Ensemble	www.facebook.com/UkulelePhilippinesEnsemble

Other Regions Around the World

Portugal

Clube da Pulga Saltitante	www.clubedapulgasaltitante.blogspot.pt/

Serbia

Ukulele Srbija	www.facebook.com/ukulelesrbija/

Singapore

Diamond Cutter Ukulele Team	www.FB.com/DCUkuleleTeam

Slovenia

Ukulele Club Slovenija	www.facebook.com/ukeklubslo

South Africa

Mother City Strummers	www.facebook.com/mothercitystrummers/

Spain

Ukelele Club Barcelona	www.barcelonaukeleleclub.blogspot.co.uk
Club del Ukulele De Madrid	www.facebook.com/clubukelelemadrid
MierKuleles	www.mierkuleles.blogspot.com.es/p/sobre-los-mierkuleles.html?m=1
Club Ukelele Valencia	www.clubukelelevalencia.com/
Barcelona Ukelele Club	www.barcelonaukeleleclub.blogspot.com

Sweden

Fagersta Ukulele Club	www.fukulele.se/
Ukelerum	www.ukulerum.org/
Ukuleleklubben	www.ukulele.nu/

Switzerland

Zurich Ukulele Meetup	www.facebook.com/zumukulele

Acknowledgements

I am a dyslexic and if it weren't for my wonderful volunteer editors, this book would have been a veritable killing ground for grammar Nazis. My editors were, Eric Zimmerman, Al Fagundes, Lissa Stephen and my wife Lily Waldman.

My writing group helped me get this book into a flow worth reading. If it weren't for them, you'd be stopped at the first run-on sentence, four letter outburst or illogical statement. My writing group members are Jonathan Eaton, Kathleen Concannon, and Rachel Hoffman, who are all fantastic writers, novelists and sounding boards for ideas. If it wasn't for our meetings, I'd be a vegan. Damn you cheese!

I also received wonderful expert contributions from, Matt Dixon, Mark Swarthout, Chontel Klobas, Gillian Altieri, Karen Snair, Gill Wales, Jim D'Ville, Bob Guz and Jen Richardson.

Finally, this book is dedicated to you, dear reader, who dares to bring the magic of music into the darkness of this world, for as Nietzsche, said, "Without music, life would be a mistake."

About Joshua Waldman

Joshua Waldman, along with his wife Lily, founded the Tigard Ukulele Group in 2015 because he wanted to play more ukulele, more often with his neighbors. Starting with seven people in his living room, the Tigard Ukulele Group now hosts up to 30 people each week, plays concerts and hosts several workshops each year. Joshua Waldman is also the author of *Job Searching with Social Media For Dummies*, in 2012, and runs a successful career blog called, CareerEnlightenment.com.

Feel free to contact the author directly at *joshua (at) tigardukes.com*

Join Other Group Leaders

As a reader of this book, I'd like to invite you to join our online community of other uke group leaders. Here we will share ideas, inspire each other and help keep up the momentum. Knowing you are not alone in your efforts can be cathartic.

I'll be sending you updates from this book as well as news and events relevant specifically to group leadership.

You can get instructions to join our online community by going here: http://www.tigardukes.com/leaders

Made in the USA
Monee, IL
11 May 2025

17254363R00109